QUILT BLOCKS: ANIMALS

QUILT BLOCKS: ANIMALS
A New Collection of Designs

Trice Boerens

LARK
CRAFTS

An Imprint of Sterling Publishing Co., Inc.
New York

WWW.LARKCRAFTS.COM

Editor
Valerie Van Arsdale Shrader

Assistant Editor
Thom O'Hearn

Art Director
Megan Kirby

Art Assistant
Meagan Shirlen

Illustrator
Trice Boerens

Photographer
Steve Mann

Cover Designer
Megan Kirby

Library of Congress Cataloging-in-Publication Data

Boerens, Trice, 1956-
  45 Quilt Blocks : Animals : A New Collection of Designs / Trice Boerens. -- First Edition.
    pages cm
  Includes index.
  ISBN 978-1-60059-715-2
  1. Patchwork--Patterns. 2. Quilting--Patterns. 3. Decoration and ornament--Animal
forms. I. Title. II. Title: Forty Five Quilt Blocks.
  TT835.B513483 2011
  746.46--dc22

                              2010048639

10 9 8 7 6 5 4 3 2 1

First Edition

Published by Lark Crafts
An Imprint of Sterling Publishing Co., Inc.
387 Park Avenue South, New York, NY 10016

Text © 2011, Trice Boerens
Photography © 2011, Lark Crafts, an Imprint of Sterling Publishing Co., Inc.
Illustrations © 2011, Trice Boerens

Distributed in Canada by Sterling Publishing,
c/o Canadian Manda Group, 165 Dufferin Street
Toronto, Ontario, Canada M6K 3H6

Distributed in the United Kingdom by GMC Distribution Services,
Castle Place, 166 High Street, Lewes, East Sussex, England BN7 1XU

Distributed in Australia by Capricorn Link (Australia) Pty Ltd.,
P.O. Box 704, Windsor, NSW 2756 Australia

If you have questions or comments about this book, please contact:
Lark Crafts
67 Broadway
Asheville, NC 28801
828-253-0467

Manufactured in China

ISBN 13: 978-1-60059-715-2

For information about custom editions, special sales, premium and corporate
purchases, please contact Sterling Special Sales Department at 800-805-5489 or
specialsales@sterlingpub.com.

For information about desk and examination copies available to college and
university professors, requests must be submitted to academic@larkbooks.com.
Our complete policy can be found at www.larkcrafts.com.

45 QUILT BLOCKS: ANIMALS

Contents   5

General Instructions   6

Quilt Blocks

1. Baby Elephant	10	
2. Baby Giraffe	11	
3. Bluebird	12	
4. Butterfly	13	
5. Chicken	14	
6. Circus Elephant	16	
7. Cow	17	
8. Crocodile	18	
9. Dancing Monkey	19	
10. Deer	20	
11. Duck	22	
12. Elephant Face	23	
13. Fox	24	
14. Frog	26	
15. Gecko	27	
16. Giraffe	28	
17. Grizzly Bear	29	
18. Happy Cat	30	
19. Happy Elephant	32	
20. Happy Monkey	33	
21. Hippo	34	
22. Horse	36	

23. Kangaroo	38
24. Lamb	40
25. Little Bear	41
26. Little Chick	42
27. Mouse	43
28. Owl	44
29. Panda	46
30. Puppy	48
31. Rabbit	49
32. Raccoon	50
33. Scotty Dog	52
34. Sitting Monkey	53
35. Sitting Cat	54
36. Snake	56
37. Squirrel	57
38. Stag	58
39. Standing Cat	60
40. Standing Dog	61
41. Standing Hippo	62
42. Standing Lion	64
43. Tiger	66
44. Whale	68
45. White Rabbit	70

Templates   72

Metric Chart   112

Index   112

General Instructions

Fabric Selection
Soft fabrics that are 100-percent cotton will work best for piecing and appliqué. Use the suggested fabric colors or alter the look of your block by choosing your own palette. If you stir patterned fabric into the mix, select small-scale designs for small template pieces.

Consider both hue and value in your selections (fig. 4). The hue describes where the color falls on the color wheel; it can be pure chroma, tinted with white, or dulled with gray (fig. 1). The value describes its degree of lightness or darkness (fig. 2).

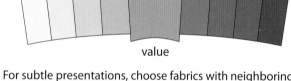

fig. 1

fig. 2

For subtle presentations, choose fabrics with neighboring hues and similar values (fig. 3). For blocks that snap, crackle, and pop, mix together contrasting hues and values (fig. 4).

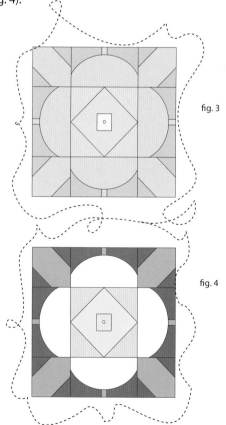

fig. 3

fig. 4

Fabric Preparation
Make sure that your selected fabrics are colorfast, and then hand wash, dry, and press them before you begin. This will preshrink the fibers and provide you with flat working materials.

Marking Tools
You can draw fine- or medium-width lines with air-soluble marking pens. The lines will be visible for a few hours and then will disappear. Water-soluble markers are similar but the lines remain until you spritz or dab them with water. Use air or water-soluble pens to mark lines for the embroidery details. For the piecing shapes, you can use the air or water-soluble markers, a #3 pencil, or a chalk pencil.

Template Preparation
Make templates from vellum paper or from lightweight polyester film, using the diagrams in the book. Enlarge the diagram as required, place the template material on the diagram, and trace around the outside edge. Cut along the marked line. Then reverse the template and place it on the wrong side of the fabric. Align the longest side of the template with the fabric grain and hold in place. Draw around the shape with a marking pen or pencil and cut along the marked line (fig. 5). The seam allowance is represented by the interior broken lines on the diagram and is ¼" wide for the pieced shapes.

Alternatively, some quilters believe that the piecing process is more accurate if you mark the finished shape and then add the seam allowance as you cut the fabric, allowing you to sew along the marked lines. For this method, place the template material on the diagram and trace along the interior broken line. Cut out the template shape, reverse it, and place it on the wrong side of the fabric. Draw around the shape with a marking pen or pencil. Then cut around the shape ¼" from the marked line to add the seam allowance (fig. 6).

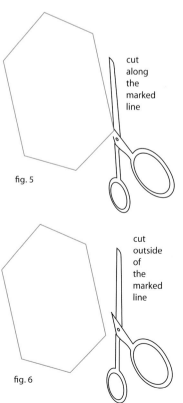

cut along the marked line

fig. 5

cut outside of the marked line

fig. 6

Machine Piecing

Pin the right sides of the pieces together and carefully feed them under the presser foot, removing the pins as you sew. Trim the threads and press each seam after sewing. At intersections, press the matching seams in opposing directions (fig. 7). Then pin the sections together with the fabric ridges pressed against each other.

Inset Seams

When joining shapes at an angle, start and stop the seams ¼" from the fabric edges (fig. 8). So the block lies flat, the stitching lines at the ends of the seams should meet but not overlap. Individual block instructions will also include this direction when required.

If you have to adjust the seam, unpick it by pulling on the bobbin thread.

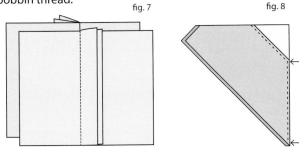

fig. 7   fig. 8

Mitered Corners

The diagonal lines of mitered corners add a jaunty angle to block designs and a crisp finish to borders. Starting and stopping ¼" from the fabric edges, sew the strips to the adjoining sides (fig. 9).

Aligning the strip edges, fold the block diagonally. Starting and stopping ¼" from the fabric edges, sew a diagonal seam at the corner (fig. 10).

Trim the excess fabric from the corner. Being careful not to cut through the seam, clip through all layers at the seam intersection (fig. 11).

Open the seam and place the block faceup on your work surface. The three seams should meet but not overlap (fig. 12).

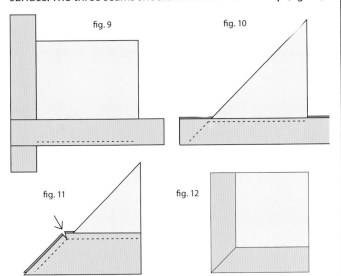

fig. 9   fig. 10

fig. 11   fig. 12

Small Triangles

When making small isosceles triangles where the two equal sides form a 90° angle (fig. 13), it is easier and more accurate to sew together pieces with square corners. Align the corners of the pieces and pin in place. Sew together along the diagonal stitching line (fig. 14). Trim the excess fabric from the corner (fig. 15). Note that this technique is *not* used when joining large triangles or those with different corner angles.

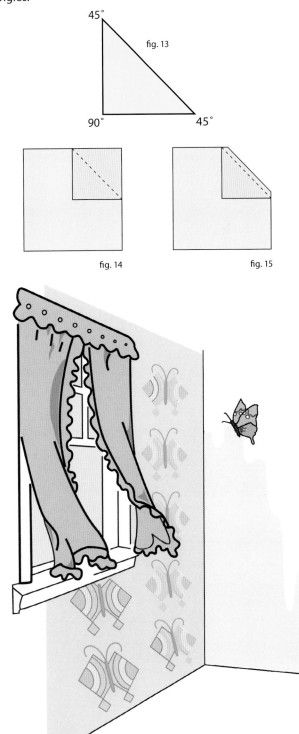

45°

fig. 13

90°   45°

fig. 14   fig. 15

Log Cabin Border

A Log Cabin border is built with four matching strips that are offset at the corners. Begin by matching the bottom edge of the first strip to the bottom edge of the square center. Starting and stopping ¼" from the fabric edges, sew the strip to the square (fig. 16).

Sew the second strip to the adjoining side (fig. 17).

Sew the third strip to the square (fig. 18).

Starting and stopping ¼" from the fabric edges, sew the last strip to the square (fig. 19).

Realign the first and the last strips and, starting and stopping ¼" from the fabric edges, sew them together at the corner (fig. 20).

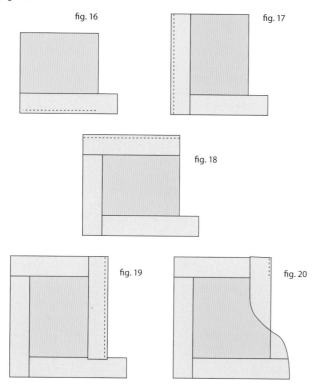

fig. 16
fig. 17
fig. 18
fig. 19
fig. 20

Hand Appliqué

Appliqués sit on top of the background fabric and provide easy and eye-catching embellishment. More flexible than piecing, appliqués can be straight or curved.

You will need a long, fine needle (#11 or #12 sharp), straight pins, scissors, and all-purpose sewing thread. Being careful not to cut through the fold lines, snip short perpendicular slits around and inside any curves (fig. 21), and pin the shape in place.

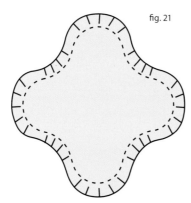

fig. 21

At your starting point, turn the fabric under at the broken line and finger press. For righties, work from right to left and slipstitch the shape to the background with close and even stitches. Lefties will do the opposite.

Work in small sections and use your needle to turn the edge under 1" ahead of your last stitch. When you reach a corner or a point, trim the tip before folding the edge under. This will eliminate bulk and allow the shape to lie flat. Knot the thread ends on the wrong side of the fabric to secure.

Curve Patch Piecing

A pieced block that is composed of straight lines and sharp angles can be softened with the introduction of a gentle arc. This is trickier than joining two straight sides, so baste rather than pin the pieces together. Being careful not to cut through the stitching lines, cut perpendicular slits along the curved edges of the cut shapes (fig. 22).

Match one concave shape to one convex shape. Then start in the middle and baste the shapes together along the marked lines with a running stitch. It will be necessary to realign and match the marked lines after every two or three stitches (fig. 23).

Flip the block over and work from the center to the opposite edge. Carefully machine stitch along the top of the basting stitches. Remove the basting stitches and press the pieced shape flat (fig. 24).

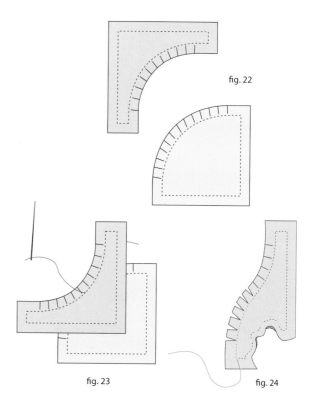

fig. 22
fig. 23
fig. 24

Embroidery

To add embroidered embellishments, use a sharp embroidery needle and two strands of floss. Knot the thread ends on the wrong side of the fabric to secure.

The embroidery designs specific to each project are included in the Templates section beginning on page 72.

Running Stitch
1. Bring the needle up through the fabric and stitch evenly in an over/under pattern.

Satin Stitch
1. Bring the needle up through the fabric at A, and back down at B.

2. Make parallel stitches that fill the desired area.

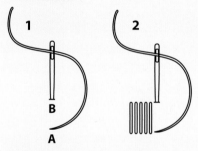

Cross Stitch
1. Bring the needle up through the fabric at A, and back down at B.

2. Then up at C and down at D.

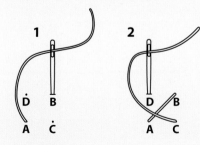

Long Stitch
1. Bring the needle up through the fabric at A, and back down at B.

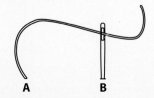

Couched Stitch
1. Secure the floss with a series of stitches.

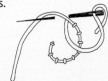

Back Stitch
1. Bring the needle up through the fabric at A, down at B, and back up at C.

2. Working right to left, insert the needle at the end of the preceding stitch and repeat.

3. Continue stitching along the marked line.

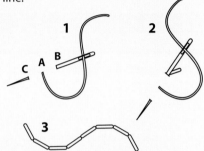

Wrapped Back Stitch
1. Refer to the Back Stitch diagrams and stitch along the marked line. Bring the needle up through the fabric at the end of the stitched line. Slide the needle under the first stitch and pull the floss through.

2. Working right to left, wrap the floss around each stitch.

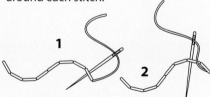

Stem Stitch
1. Bring the needle up through the fabric at A, down at B, and back up at C.

2. Working left to right, insert the needle at D and back up at the end of the preceding stitch.

3. Continue stitching along the marked line.

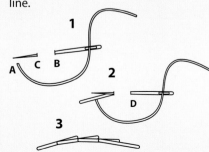

Blanket Stitch
1. Bring the needle up through the fabric at A, down at B, and back up at C.

2. Working left to right, continue along the turned edge or the marked line.

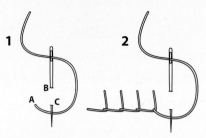

Chain Stitch
1. Bring the needle up through the fabric at A, down at B, and back up at C.

2. Working right to left, insert the needle in the center of the preceding stitch and repeat. Continue along the marked line.

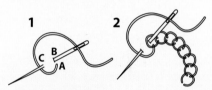

Spider Web Rose
1. Refer to the Long Stitch and make five spokes.

2. Bring the needle up at the center and in a counterclockwise direction, thread the needle over and under the spokes to make a tight coil.

3. On the outside edge of the coil, insert the needle from the front to the back and knot to secure.

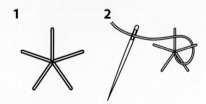

French Knot
1. Bring the needle up through the fabric, and wrap the floss around its center. Enlarge the size of the knot by wrapping the needle twice.

2. Push the needle through the fabric close to the point it emerged and pull it to the back.

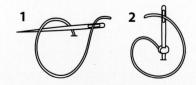

BABY ELEPHANT

Block Sizes
6³/₄" x 6" or 8¹/₂" x 7¹/₂"

Templates on page 72; enlarge 250%

Fabrics and Materials
Black solid, light gray solid, orange print, dark gray solid, and white solid

Coordinating thread

Teal embroidery floss

Cut the Pieces
1. From the black solid, cut two pieces each from Templates A, K, L, and M. Cut one piece each from Templates H and I. Reverse Template I and cut one additional piece.

2. From the light gray solid, cut one piece each from Templates B and F. (Note that the seam allowance for Template F is narrow. Because the shape is appliquéd, the edge is turned under at the broken line.)

3. From the orange print, cut two pieces from Template C and one piece from Template J. Reverse Template J and cut one additional piece.

4. From the dark gray print, cut one piece from Template D and two pieces from Template G.

5. From the white solid, cut one piece from Template E. Reverse Template E and cut one additional piece. (Note that the seam allowance is narrow. Because the shape is appliquéd, the edge is turned under at the broken line.)

Assemble the Block
1. Refer to the General Instructions for Small Triangles (page 7) as necessary throughout and sew the A squares to the B shape. (Figure 1)

2. Sew the C squares to the D shape. (Figure 2)

3. Refer to the General Instructions for Hand Appliqué (page 8) and sew the E and F shapes to the C/D shape. (Figure 3)

4. Sew the G shapes to the H shape. Sew the pieced shapes together. (Figure 4)

5. Sew one I triangle to one J shape. Sew one K square to the J shape. (Figure 5)

6. Sew one L and M shape to the pieced shape. (Figure 6) Repeat steps 5 and 6 to make a reverse pieced shape.

7. Sew the pieced shapes together to complete the block. (Figure 7)

8. Refer to the General Instructions for Embroidery (page 9) and stitch the embroidered details to the block. (Figure 8)

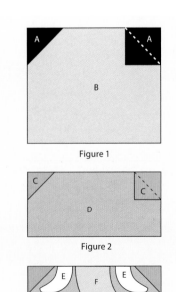

Figure 1

Figure 2

Figure 3

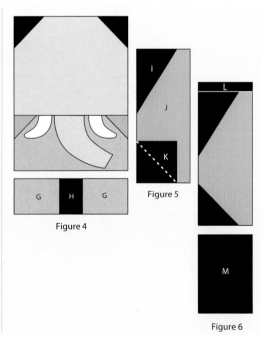

Figure 4

Figure 5

Figure 6

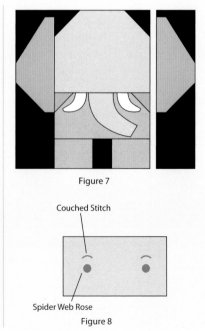

Figure 7

Couched Stitch

Spider Web Rose

Figure 8

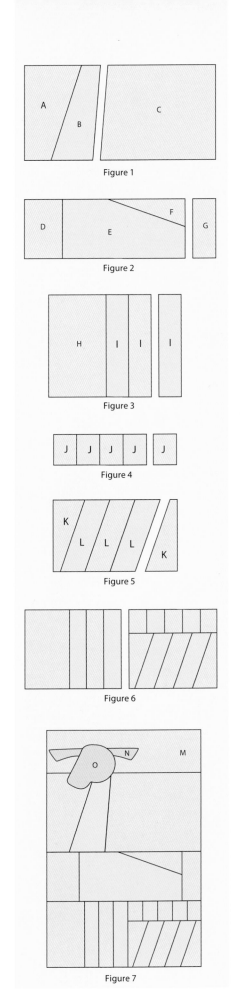

Figure 1

Figure 2

Figure 3

Figure 4

Figure 5

Figure 6

Figure 7

Block Sizes

6" x 9" or 7" x 10$\frac{1}{2}$"

Templates on page 73; enlarge 250%

Fabrics and Materials

Pink print, yellow print, gold solid, and gold print

Coordinating thread

Tan, dark blue, and light blue embroidery floss

Cut the Pieces

1. From the pink print, cut one piece each from Templates A, C, D, F, G, H, I, L, and M; three pieces from Template J; and two pieces from Template K.

2. From the yellow print, cut one piece each from Templates B and E. Cut two pieces each from Templates I, J, and L.

3. From the gold solid, cut one piece from Template N. From the gold print, cut one piece from Template O. (Note that the seam allowances for Templates N and O are narrow. Because the shapes are appliquéd, the edges are turned under at the broken line.)

Assemble the Block

1. Sew the A, B, and C shapes together. (Figure 1)

2. Sew the D, E, and F shapes together. Sew the G shape to the pieced shape. (Figure 2)

3. Sew the H shape to the I shapes. (Figure 3)

4. Sew the J shapes together. (Figure 4)

5. Sew the K and L shapes together. (Figure 5)

6. Sew the pieced shapes from steps 3, 4, and 5 together. (Figure 6)

7. Sew the remaining pieced shapes together. Sew the M shape to the pieced shapes to complete the block. Refer to the General Instructions for Hand Appliqué (page 8), and noting overlaps, sew the N and O shapes to the block. (Figure 7)

8. Refer to the General Instructions for Embroidery (page 9), and stitch the embroidered details to the block. (Figure 8) Add a Running Stitch around the giraffe head and body.

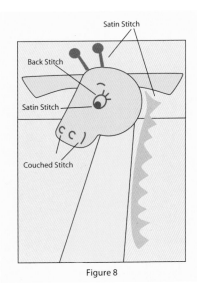

Figure 8

3 BLUEBIRD

Block Sizes

6¹/₂" square or 8" square

Templates on page 74; enlarge 250%

Fabrics and Materials

Blue print, ivory mottle, and pink mottle

Coordinating thread

Pink, yellow, and gold embroidery floss

Cut the Pieces

1. From the blue print, cut one piece each from Templates B, E, G, and J.

2. From the ivory mottle, cut two pieces each from Templates A and H. Cut one piece each from Templates C, D, I, and K.

3. From the pink mottle, cut one piece from Template F.

Assemble the Block

1. Refer to the General Instructions for Small Triangles (page 7) as necessary throughout and sew two A squares to the B shape. (Figure 1)

2. Sew C and D shapes to the piece created in step 1. (Figure 2)

3. Sew the E, F and G shapes together. (Figure 3)

4. Sew the H squares to the pieced shape from step 3. (Figure 4)

5. Sew the I, J, and K shapes together. (Figure 5)

6. Sew the pieced shapes together to complete the block. (Figure 6)

7. Refer to the General Instructions for Embroidery (page 9) and stitch the embroidered details to the block. (Figure 7 and Figure 8)

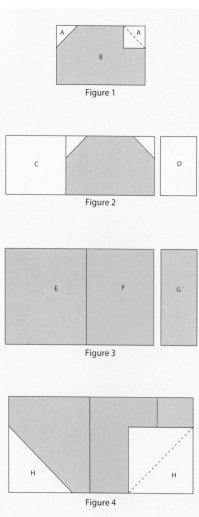

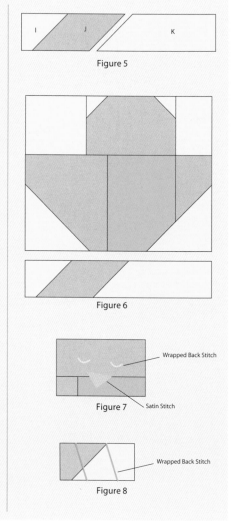

BUTTERFLY

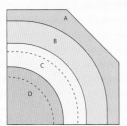

Figure 1

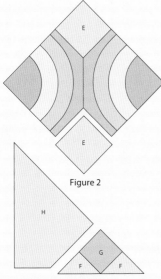

Figure 2

Figure 3

Block Sizes
6^1/$_2$" square or 8" square

Templates on page 75; enlarge 250%

Fabrics and Materials
Blue print, dark pink print, melon solid, rust solid, light pink print, and burgundy solid

Coordinating thread

Red embroidery floss

Cut the Pieces
1. From the blue print, cut one piece from Template A. Reverse Template A and cut one additional piece. Cut two pieces from Template G.

Note that the seam allowances are narrow for Templates B, C, D, and J. Because these shapes are appliquéd, their edges are turned under at the broken line.

2. From the dark pink print, cut two pieces from Template B.

3. From the melon solid, cut two pieces from Template C.

4. From the rust solid, cut two pieces from Template D.

5. From the light pink print, cut two pieces each from Templates E and I. Cut four pieces each from Template F and one piece from Template H. Reverse Template H and cut one additional piece.

6. From the burgundy solid, cut one piece from Template J.

Assemble the Block
1. Refer to the General Instructions for Hand Appliqué (page 8) and, noting overlaps, stitch the B, C, and D shapes to the A shape. (Figure 1) Repeat to make a reverse appliqué shape.

2. Refer to the General Instructions for Inset Seams (page 7) and starting and stopping ^{1}/$_4$" from the fabric edges, sew the A shapes together. Sew the E squares to the pieced shape. (Figure 2)

3. Sew the F triangles to the G square. Sew the F/G triangle to the H shape. (Figure 3) Repeat to make one additional shape that is the reverse.

4. Sew the I triangles and the pieced triangles from step 3 to the square center to complete the block. Refer to the General Instructions for Hand Appliqué (page 8) and sew the J shape to the block. (Figure 4)

5. Refer to the General Instructions for Embroidery (page 9) and stitch the embroidered details to the block. (Figure 5)

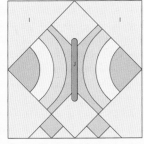

Figure 4

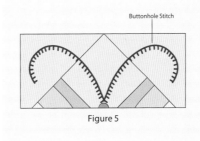

Buttonhole Stitch

Figure 5

CHICKEN

5

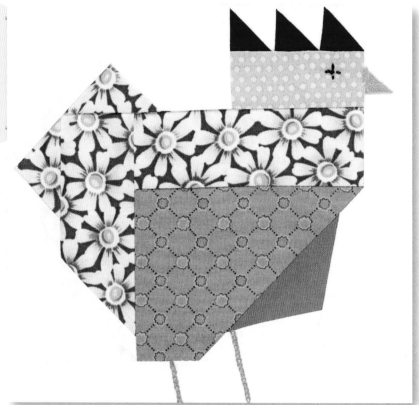

Block Sizes
7" square or 8³/₄" square

Templates on page 76; enlarge 250%

Fabrics and Materials
Burgundy solid, white solid, blue polka dot, blue floral, rust solid, and lavender print

Coordinating thread

Blue, turquoise, and orange embroidery floss

Cut the Pieces
1. From the burgundy solid, cut three pieces from Template A.

2. From the white solid, cut three pieces from Template A. Cut one piece each from Templates D, F, J, K, L, M and N. Reverse Template F and cut one additional piece.

3. From the blue polka dot, cut one piece from Template B.

4. From the blue floral, cut two pieces from Template C. Cut one piece each from Templates H and I.

5. From the rust solid, cut one piece from Template E.

6. From the lavender print, cut one piece from Template G.

Assemble the Block
1. Refer to the General Instructions for Small Triangles (page 7) as necessary throughout and sew the A squares together. (Figure 1) Repeat to make two additional pieced squares.

2. Sew the pieced squares together. (Figure 2)

3. Sew the B shape to the pieced strip. Sew the C shape to the D shape. Sew the pieced shapes together. (Figure 3)

4. Sew one F shape to the E triangle. Trim the end. (Figure 4)

5. Sew the remaining F shape to the pieced shape from step 4. Sew the G and H shapes to the E/F shape. (Figure 5)

6. Sew the I and J shapes together. Sew the I/J shape to the pieced shape. (Figure 6)

7. Sew the C and K shapes together. Sew the C/K shape to the pieced shapes from steps 3 and 5. (Figure 7)

8. Sew the L, M, and N shapes to the pieced shape to complete the block. (Figure 8)

9. Refer to the General Instructions for Embroidery (page 9) and stitch the embroidered details to the block. (Figure 9 and Figure 10)

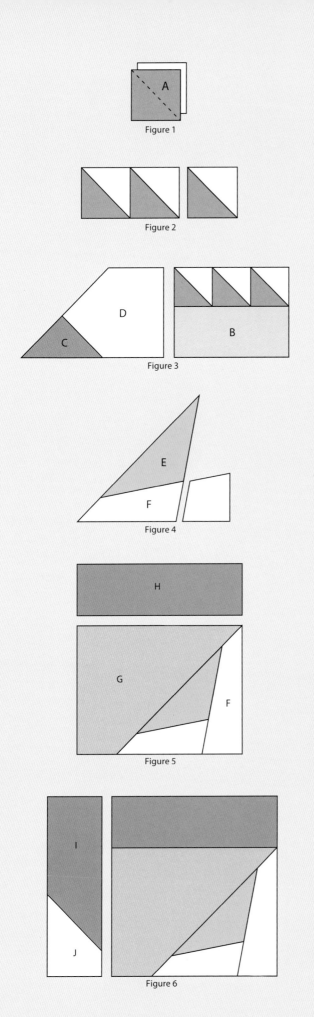

Figure 1

Figure 2

Figure 3

Figure 4

Figure 5

Figure 6

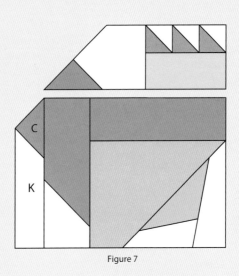

Figure 7

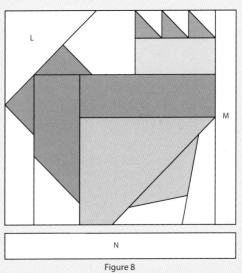

Figure 8

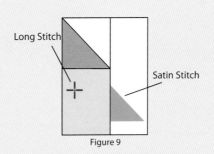

Long Stitch

Satin Stitch

Figure 9

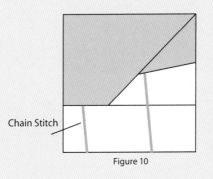

Chain Stitch

Figure 10

CIRCUS ELEPHANT

Block Sizes
6$\frac{1}{2}$" square or 8$\frac{1}{2}$" square

Templates on page 77; enlarge 250%

Fabrics and Materials
Yellow solid, melon solid, blue solid, red check, and brown solid

Coordinating thread

Tan and navy embroidery floss

Cut the Pieces
1. From the yellow solid, cut three pieces from Template A. Cut one piece each from Templates D, E, H, and K. Cut two pieces from Template I.

2. From the melon solid, cut four pieces from Template A and one piece from Template C.

3. From the blue solid, cut one piece each from Templates B, F, G, and L.

4. From the red check, cut four pieces from Template A.

5. From the brown solid, cut one piece each from Templates A, J, and L. Cut two pieces from Template D.

Assemble the Block
1. Refer to the General Instructions for Small Triangles (page 7) as necessary throughout and sew one yellow A square and one melon A square to the B shape. (Figure 1)

2. Sew two red A squares and one melon A square to the C shape. Sew the D shapes together and then to the pieced shape. (Figure 2)

3. Sew one yellow A square and one melon A square to the E shape. (Figure 3)

4. Sew the A squares to the D shape. Sew the F shape to the pieced shape. (Figure 4)

5. Sew one yellow A square to the G shape. Sew the brown A square to the H shape. Sew these pieced shapes together. (Figure 5)

6. Sew the I shapes to the J shape. (Figure 6)

7. Sew the pieced shapes from steps 5 and 6 to the K square. (Figure 7)

8. Sew the L shapes together. Sew the L/L shape to the pieced shape from step 7. Trim the end. (Figure 8)

9. Sew the pieced shapes together to complete the block. (Figure 9)

10. Refer to the General Instructions for Embroidery (page 9) and stitch the embroidered details to the block. (Figure 10 and Figure 11)

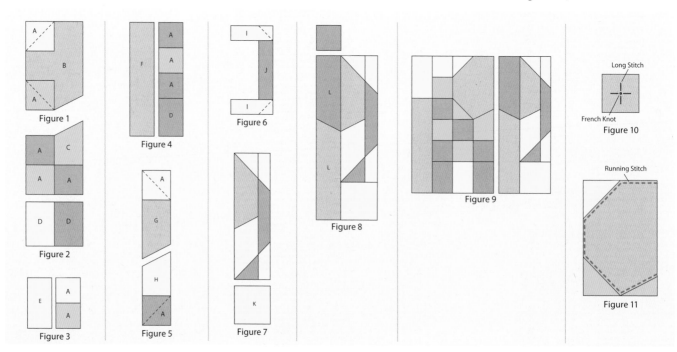

Figure 1
Figure 2
Figure 3
Figure 4
Figure 5
Figure 6
Figure 7
Figure 8
Figure 9
Figure 10
Long Stitch
French Knot
Running Stitch
Figure 11

Block Sizes

6 ¹/₄" square or 7 ¹/₂" square

Templates on page 78; enlarge 250%

Fabrics and Materials

Brown solid, lavender solid, yellow solid, red check, white print, gold solid, and pink solid

Coordinating thread

Cream, brown, orange, light green, and dark green embroidery floss

Cut the Pieces

1. From the brown solid, cut two pieces each from Templates A and E. Cut one piece each from Templates D, G, and I.

2. From the lavender solid, cut one piece from Template B.

3. From the yellow solid, cut one piece from each from Templates F, H, and I. Cut two pieces from Template C.

4. From the red check, cut four pieces from Template N. Note that the seam allowances are narrow for Templates J through M. Because these shapes are appliquéd, their edges are turned under at the broken line.

5. From the white print, cut one piece each from Templates J and K.

6. From the gold solid, cut one piece from Template L.

7. From the pink solid, cut two pieces from Template M.

Assemble the Block

1. Refer to the General Instructions for Small Triangles (page 7) and sew the A squares to the B shape. Refer to the General Instructions for Inset Seams (page 7) and starting and stopping ¹/₄" from the fabric edges, sew the C shapes to the B shape.

2. Starting and stopping ¹/₄" from the fabric edges, sew the D shape to the pieced shape from step 1. (Figure 2)

3. Sew the E shapes to the F shape. (Figure 3)

4. Sew the G shape to the H shape. Sew the pieced shapes together. (Figure 4)

5. Sew the I shapes together. Sew the pieced shapes together and trim the end. (Figure 5)

6. Refer to the General Instruction for Hand Appliqué' (page 8) and noting overlaps, sew the J,K,L, and M shapes to the block. Refer to the General Instructions for the Log Cabin Border (page 8) and sew the N strips around the square center to complete the block. (Figure 7)

7. Refer to the General Instructions for Embroidery (page 9) and stitch the embroidered details to the block. (Figure 7 and Figure 8)

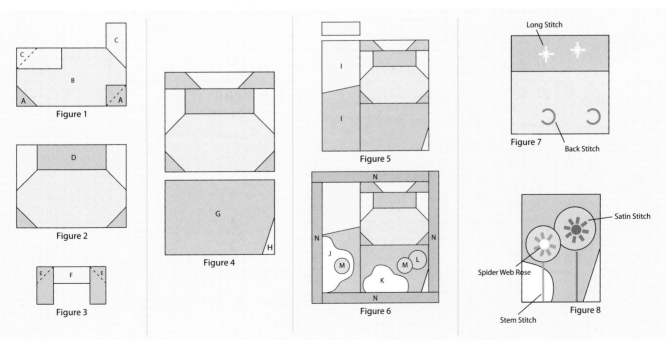

Figure 1

Figure 2

Figure 3

Figure 4

Figure 5

Figure 6

Figure 7

Figure 8

CROCODILE

8

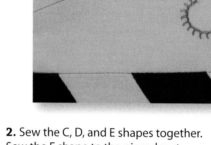

Block Sizes
7" x 6¹/₄" or 8¹/₂" x 7¹/₂"

Templates on page 79; enlarge 250%

Fabrics and Materials
Green solid and purple solid

Coordinating thread

Green and white embroidery floss

Cut the Pieces
1. From the green solid, cut one piece each from Templates A, C, D, and J. (Note that the seam allowance for Template J is narrow. Because the shape is appliquéd, the edge is turned under at the broken line.) Cut four pieces from Template G and two pieces from Template L.

2. From the purple solid, cut one piece each from Templates B, E, F, H, I, K, and M. Cut three pieces from Template G.

Assemble the Block
1. Sew the A shape to the B triangle. (Figure 1)

2. Sew the C, D, and E shapes together. Sew the F shape to the pieced rectangle. (Figure 2)

3. Sew the pieced shapes from steps 1 and 2 together. (Figure 3)

4. Sew the G triangles together. Sew the H shape to the pieced strip. (Figure 4)

5. Sew the pieced G/H strip to the pieced shape and trim the end. (Figure 5)

6. Refer to the General Instructions for Hand Appliqué (page 8) and sew the J shape to the I shape. (Figure 6)

7. Sew the K, L, and M shapes together. (Figure 7)

8. Sew the pieced shapes to the square center to complete the block. (Figure 8)

9. Refer to the General Instructions for Embroidery (page 9) and stitch the embroidered details to the block. (Figure 9)

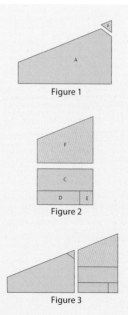

Figure 1

Figure 2

Figure 3

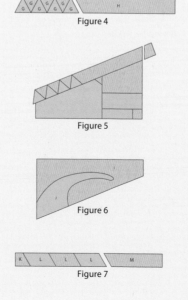

Figure 4

Figure 5

Figure 6

Figure 7

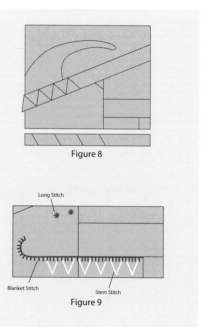

Figure 8

Figure 9

Block Sizes

6¹/₂" x 8¹/₂" or 8" x 10¹/₂"

Templates on page 80; enlarge 250%

Fabrics and Materials

White solid, gold print, brown print, purple solid, and brown solid

Coordinating thread

Light brown and dark brown embroidery floss

Cut the Pieces

1. From the white solid, cut one piece each from Templates A and J. Reverse Template J and cut one additional piece. Cut two pieces each from Templates C, D, and H. Cut four pieces from Template M.

2. From the gold print, cut one piece each from Templates B and G.

3. From the brown print, cut one piece each from Templates E, I, and K. Reverse Template K and cut one additional piece. Cut two pieces each from Templates F and N. (Note that the seam allowance for Template N is narrow. Because the shape is appliquéd, the edge is turned under at the broken line.)

4. From the purple solid, cut one piece from Template L.

5. From the brown solid, cut one piece from Template O. (Note that the seam allowance for Template O is narrow. Because the shape is appliquéd, the edge is turned under at the broken line.

Assemble the Block

1. Sew the A, B, and C shapes together. (Figure 1)

2. Refer to the General Instructions for Small Triangles (page 7) as necessary throughout and sew the D squares to the pieced rectangle. (Figure 2)

3. Sew the E, F, and G shapes together. Sew the H triangle to the I shape. Sew the pieced shapes together. (Figure 3)

4. Sew the K shapes to the H triangle. Sew the J triangles to the H/K shape. Sew the L shape to the pieced shape. (Figure 4)

5. Sew the pieced shapes together. (Figure 5)

6. Sew the M shapes to the square center to complete the block. (Figure 6)

7. Refer to the General Instructions for Hand Appliqué (page 8) and sew the N and O shapes to the block. (Figure 7) Unpick the seams and tuck the ends of the arms in to secure; whipstitch closed.

8. Refer to the General Instructions for Embroidery (page 9) and stitch the embroidered details to the block. (Figure 8)

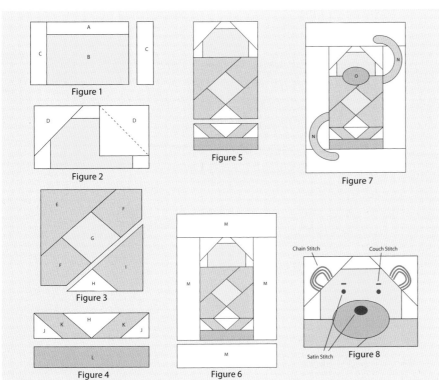

Figure 1

Figure 2

Figure 3

Figure 4

Figure 5

Figure 6

Figure 7

Chain Stitch   Couch Stitch

Satin Stitch   Figure 8

DEER

Block Sizes

7 1/4" square or 8 3/4" square

Templates on page 81; enlarge 250%

Fabrics and Materials

Navy solid, gray solid, rust solid, gold print, and tan print

Coordinating thread

Rust, red, and yellow embroidery floss

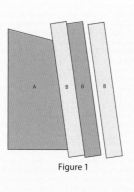

Figure 1

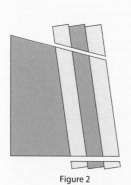

Figure 2

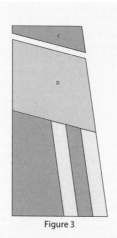

Figure 3

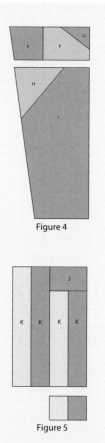

Figure 4

Figure 5

Cut the Pieces

1. From the navy solid, cut one piece each from Templates A, B, C, E, G, I, J, and N. Cut three pieces from Template K.

2. From the gray solid, cut two pieces each from Templates B and K.

3. From the rust solid, cut one piece each from Templates D, F and H.

4. From the gold print, cut one piece from Template L.

5. From the tan print, cut one piece from Template M. Reverse Template M and cut one additional piece. (Note that the seam allowance for Template M is narrow. Because the shape is appliquéd, the edge is turned under at the broken line.)

Assemble the Block

1. Sew the A shape to the B shapes. (Figure 1)

2. Trim the ends. (Figure 2)

3. Sew the C and D shapes to the pieced shape. (Figure 3)

4. Sew the E, F, and G shapes together. Sew the H and I shapes to the pieced shape. (Figure 4)

5. Sew the J and K shapes together. Trim the ends. (Figure 5)

6. Sew the K and L shapes to the pieced shape. (Figure 6)

7. Sew the pieced shapes together. (Figure 7)

8. Refer to the General Instructions for Hand Appliqué (page 8) and sew the M shapes to the N shape. (Figure 8)

9. Sew the strip to the square center to complete the block. (Figure 9)

10. Refer to the General Instructions for Embroidery (page 9) and stitch the embroidered details to the block. Add blanket stitch around the ears, cross stitch in the body, and stem stitch for the eye. (Figure 10)

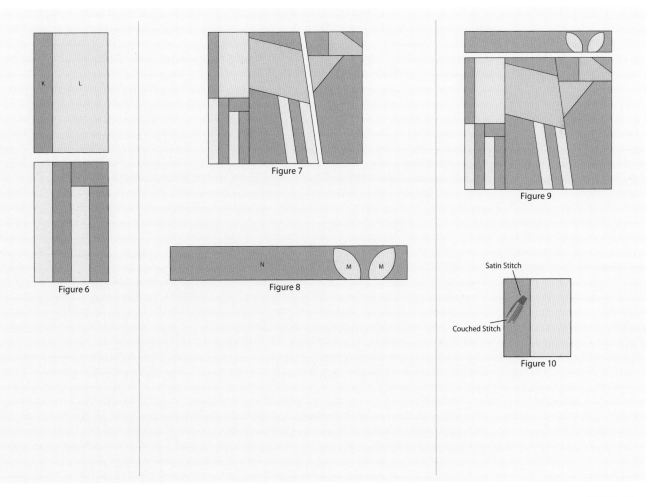

Figure 6

Figure 7

Figure 8

Figure 9

Satin Stitch

Couched Stitch

Figure 10

DUCK

Block Sizes
5½" square or 7" square

Templates on page 75; enlarge 250%

Fabrics and Materials
Gold solid, blue polka dot, and orange print

Coordinating thread

Tan and blue embroidery floss

Cut the Pieces
1. From the gold solid, cut one piece from Template A. (Note that the seam allowance is narrow. Because the shape is appliquéd, the edge is turned under at the broken line.) Cut one piece from Template E.

2. From the blue polka dot, cut one piece each from Templates B, D, C, and F.

3. From the orange print, cut one piece from Template G. (Note that the seam allowance is narrow. Because the shape is appliquéd, the edge is turned under at the broken line.)

Assemble the Block
1. Refer to the General Instructions for Hand Appliqué (page 8) and sew the A shape to the B shape. (Figure 1)

2. Refer to the General Instructions for Small Triangles (page 7) as necessary throughout and sew the C and D squares to the E shape. Sew the F triangle to the pieced shape. (Figure 2)

3. Sew the pieced shapes together to complete the block. (Figure 3)

4. Refer to the General Instructions for Hand Appliqué (page 8) and sew the G shape to the block. (Figure 4)

5. Refer to the General Instructions for Embroidery (page 9) and stitch the embroidered details to the block. (Figure 5 and Figure 6)

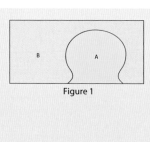

Figure 1

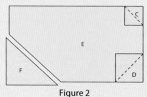

Figure 2

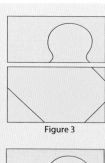

Figure 3

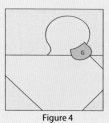

Figure 4

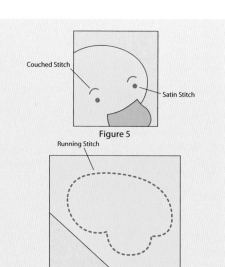

Figure 5

Figure 6

Block Sizes

7¼" square or 8¾" square

Templates on page 82; enlarge 250%

Fabrics and Materials

Gold print, gray solid, green print, and charcoal solid

Coordinating thread

Light gray, dark gray, pink, and burgundy embroidery floss

Cut the Pieces

1. From the gold print, cut one piece each from Templates A and C. Cut four pieces from Template D and two pieces from Template E.

2. From the gray solid, cut one piece each from Templates B and G. Reverse Template B and cut one additional piece.

3. From the green print, cut two pieces from Template F.

4. From the charcoal solid, cut one piece from Template H. (Note that the seam allowance is narrow. Because the shape is appliquéd, the edge is turned under at the broken line.)

Assemble the Block

1. Sew the A, B, and C shapes together. (Figure 1)

2. Sew the D triangles to the pieced shape. Refer to the General Instructions for Small Triangles (page 7) as necessary throughout and sew the E squares to the pieced shape. (Figure 2)

3. Sew the F triangles to the G shape. Sew the D triangles to the F/G shape. (Figure 3)

4. Sew the pieced shapes together to complete the block. (Figure 4)

5. Refer to the General Instructions for Hand Appliqué (page 8) and sew the H shape to the block. (Figure 5)

6. Refer to the General Instructions for Embroidery (page 9) and stitch the embroidered details to the block. (Figure 6) Add blanket stitch around each ear.

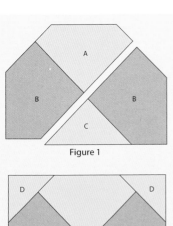
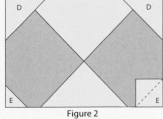

Figure 1

Figure 2

Figure 3

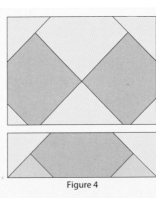
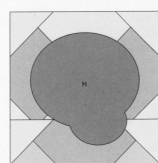

Figure 4

Figure 5

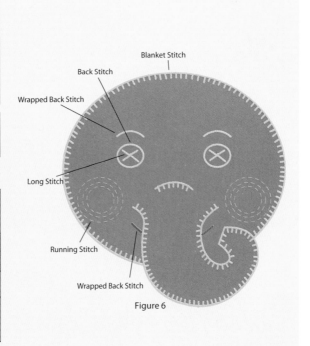

Figure 6

Blanket Stitch

Back Stitch

Wrapped Back Stitch

Long Stitch

Running Stitch

Wrapped Back Stitch

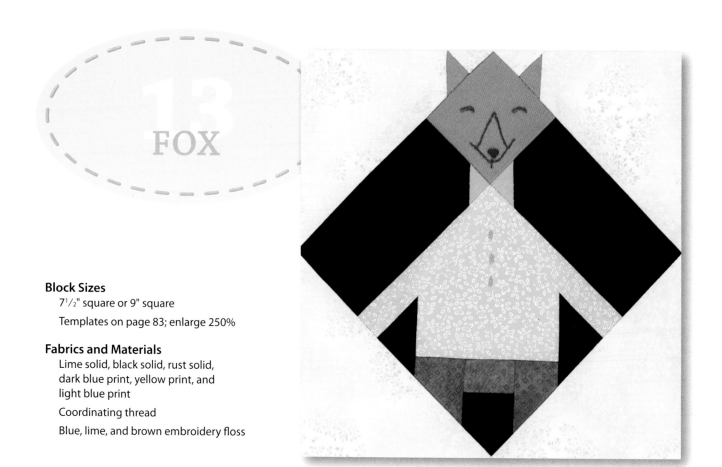

13 FOX

Block Sizes

7½" square or 9" square

Templates on page 83; enlarge 250%

Fabrics and Materials

Lime solid, black solid, rust solid, dark blue print, yellow print, and light blue print

Coordinating thread

Blue, lime, and brown embroidery floss

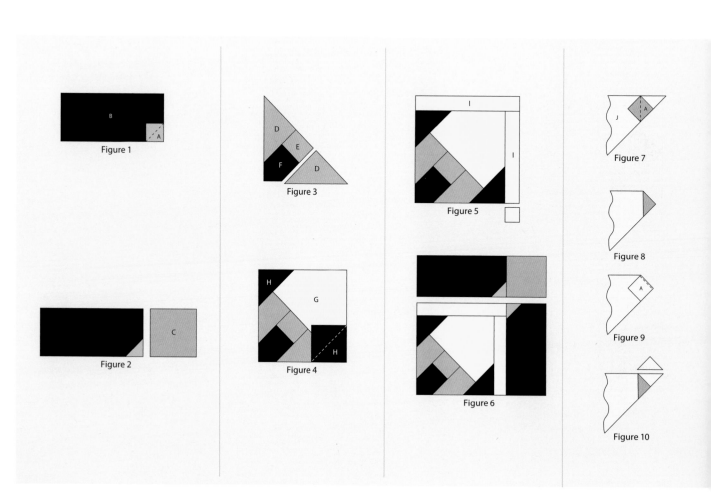

Figure 1

Figure 2

Figure 3

Figure 4

Figure 5

Figure 6

Figure 7

Figure 8

Figure 9

Figure 10

Cut the Pieces

1. From the lime solid, cut two pieces from Template A.

2. From the black solid, cut two pieces each from Templates B and H. Cut one piece from Template F.

3. From the rust solid, cut two pieces from Template A and one piece from Template C.

4. From the dark blue print, cut two pieces from Template D and one piece from Template E.

5. From the yellow print, cut one piece from Template G and two pieces from Template I.

6. From the light blue print, cut four pieces from Template J and two pieces from Template A.

Assemble the Block

1. Refer to the General Instructions for Small Triangles (page 7) as necessary throughout and sew the A square to the B shape. (Figure 1) Repeat to make an additional A/B shape that is the reverse.

2. Sew the C square to one A/B shape. (Figure 2)

3. Sew the E and F shapes together. Sew the E/F shape to the D shapes. (Figure 3)

4. Sew the G shape to the pieced shape you created in Step 3. Sew the H squares to the pieced shape. (Figure 4)

5. Sew the I strips to the pieced shape. Trim the end. (Figure 5)

6. Sew the pieced shapes together. (Figure 6)

7. Sew the rust A square to the J triangle along the marked line. Trim the corners of the A and J shapes and fold the A corner over with the right-side up. (Figure 7 and Figure 8)

8. Sew one blue A square to the A/J shape. (Figure 9) Trim the corner of the A square. (Figure 10) Repeat to make a reversed pieced shape.

9. Sew the pieced triangles and the J triangles to the square center to complete the block. (Figure 11)

10. Refer to the General Instructions for Embroidery (page 9) and stitch the embroidered details to the block. (Figure 12)

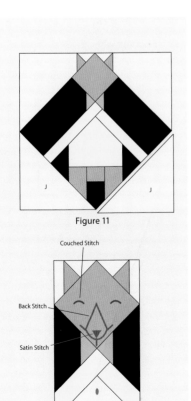

Figure 11

Couched Stitch

Back Stitch

Satin Stitch

Figure 12

14

FROG

Block Sizes

6¼" square or 7½" square

Templates on page 84; enlarge 250%

Fabrics and Materials

Pink mottle, green print, lime solid, gold print, and white solid

Coordinating thread

Brown and teal embroidery floss

Cut the Pieces

1. From the pink mottle, cut two pieces each from Templates A and D. Cut one piece each from Templates C and E. Reverse Template E and cut one additional piece. Cut three pieces from Template J.

2. From the green print, cut one piece each from Templates B, G, and F. Reverse Templates G and F and cut one additional piece from each.

3. From the lime solid, cut two pieces each from Templates I and J.

4. From the gold print, cut one piece from Template H.

5. From the white solid, cut two pieces from Template K. (Note that the seam allowance is narrow. Because the shape is appliquéd, the edge is turned under at the broken line.)

Assemble the Block

1. Refer to the General Instructions for Small Triangles (page 7) as necessary throughout and sew the A squares to the B shape. (Figure 1)

2. Sew the C and D shapes to the pieced shape. (Figure 2)

3. Sew the E, F, and G shapes together. (Figure 3) Repeat to make a reverse pieced shape.

4. Sew the I shapes to the H shape. Sew the pieced shapes created in step 3 to the I/H shape. (Figure 4)

5. Sew the J shapes together. (Figure 5)

6. Sew all the pieced shapes together to complete the block. (Figure 6)

7. Refer to the General Instructions for Hand Appliqué (page 8) and sew the K shapes to the block. (Figure 7)

8. Refer to the General Instructions for Embroidery (page 9) and stitch the embroidered details to the block. (Figure 8)

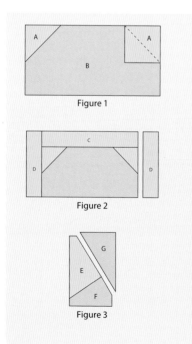

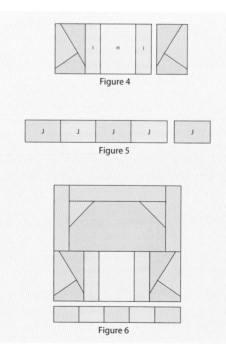

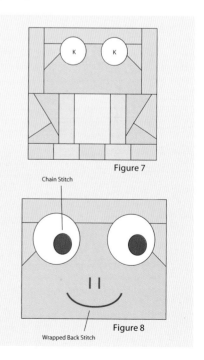

GECKO

Block Sizes

6" x 7¼" or 7½" x 9"

Templates are on page 85; enlarge 250%

Fabrics and Materials

Violet print, green solid, green print, and gold print

Coordinating thread

Navy embroidery floss

Cut the Pieces

1. From the violet print, cut three pieces each from Templates A and F. Cut two pieces each from Templates C and L. Cut one piece each from Templates G, H, and I; and cut four pieces from Template J.

2. From the green solid, cut one piece each from Templates A, B, E, F, and G.

3. From the green print, cut two pieces from Template D.

4. From the gold print, cut four pieces from Template K.

Assemble the Block

1. Refer to the General Instructions for Small Triangles (page 7) as necessary throughout and sew the A squares to the B shape. (Figure 1)

2. Sew the C shapes to the A/B block. (Figure 2)

3. Sew the violet F squares to the E shape. (Figure 3)

4. Sew the A squares together, the F squares together, and the G triangles together to make three violet/green pieced squares. (Figure 4)

5. Sew the H shape to the A/A square from step 4. Sew the F/F and G/G squares to the pieced shape. (Figure 5)

6. Sew the I shape to the pieced shape from step 5. (Figure 6)

7. Sew the D shapes to the pieced shapes. (Figure 7)

8. Sew two J, two K, and one L shape together. Repeat to make an additional pieced strip. (Figure 8)

9. Sew the strips to the square center to complete the block. Trim the ends. (Figure 9)

10. Refer to the General Instructions for Embroidery (page 9) and stitch the embroidered details to the block. (Figure 10)

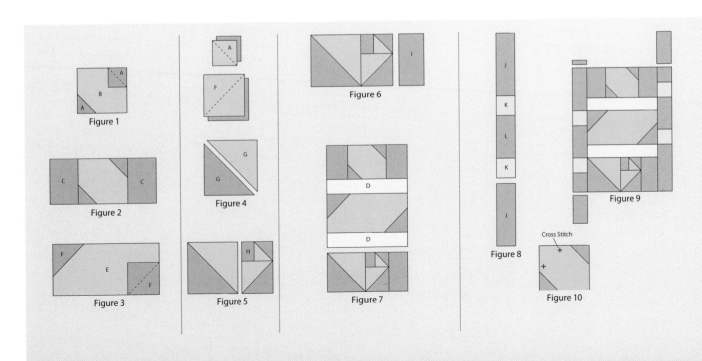

Figure 1
Figure 2
Figure 3
Figure 4
Figure 5
Figure 6
Figure 7
Figure 8
Figure 9
Figure 10
Cross Stitch

Block Sizes

7¼" square or 9" square

Templates on page 86; enlarge 250%

Fabrics and Materials

Blue solid, yellow solid, white solid, and yellow print

Coordinating thread

Brown embroidery floss

Cut the Pieces

1. From the blue solid, cut one piece each from Templates A, F, H, G, I, K, and L. Cut three pieces from Template C.

2. From the yellow solid, cut one piece each from Templates B, D, and J. Reverse Template J and cut one additional piece. Cut four pieces from Template C.

3. From the white solid, cut one piece from Template E.

4. From the yellow print, cut one piece from Template M. (Note that the seam allowance is narrow. Because the shape is appliquéd, the edge is turned under at the broken line.)

Assemble the Block

1. Refer to the General Instructions for Small Triangles (page 7) and sew the A square to the B shape. (Figure 1)

2. Sew the C shapes together. (Figure 2)

3. Sew the D, E, and F shapes together. (Figure 3)

4. Sew the G and H shapes to the pieced shape created in step 3. (Figure 4)

5. Sew the I, J, and K shapes together. (Figure 5)

6. Sew the L shape to the pieced shape from step 5. Trim the corner. (Figure 6)

7. Sew the pieced shapes together to complete the block. (Figure 7)

8. Refer to the General Instructions for Hand Appliqué (page 8) and sew the M shape to the block. (Figure 8)

9. Refer to the General Instructions for Embroidery (page 9) and stitch the embroidered details to the block. (Figure 9 and Figure 10)

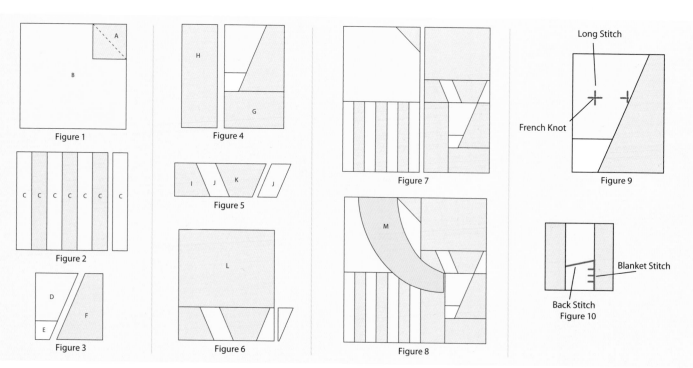

Block Sizes
7¹/₂ x 7" or 9 x 8³/₈"

Templates on page 87; enlarge 250%

Fabrics and Materials
Pink solid, rust solid, brown solid, burgundy solid, blue check, and dark green print

Coordinating thread

Brown and orange embroidery floss

Cut the Pieces
1. From the pink solid, cut one piece each from Templates B and H. Cut three pieces from Template D and two pieces from Template F.

2. From the rust solid, cut one piece from Template A. (Note that the seam allowance is narrow. Because the shape is appliquéd, the edge is turned under at the broken line.)

3. From the brown solid, cut three pieces from Template C.

4. From the burgundy solid, cut two pieces from Template E and one piece from Template G.

5. From the blue check, cut four 1" x 8" strips for the small block or four 1¹/₈" x 8¹/₂" strips for the large block.

6. From the dark green print, cut four pieces from Template I.

Assemble the Block
1. Refer to the General Instructions for Hand Appliqué (page 8) and sew the A shape to the B shape. Sew the C shape to the A/B shape. (Figure 1)

2. Sew the D, E, and F shapes together. Sew a C shape to the pieced shape. (Figure 2) Repeat to make a second pieced shape.

3. Sew the remaining D and G shapes together. (Figure 3)

4. Sew all the pieced shapes together. Sew the H shape to the pieced shape. Trim the corners. (Figure 4)

5. Sew two blue check strips to the sides of the square center. Sew two I squares to one remaining strip; repeat to make one additional pieced strip. Sew the pieced strips to the top and bottom of the square to complete the block. (Figure 5)

6. Refer to the General Instructions for Embroidery (page 9) and stitch the embroidered details to the block. (Figure 6)

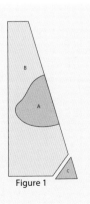

Figure 1

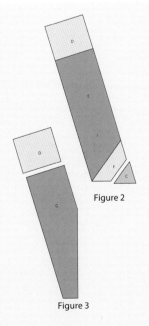

Figure 2

Figure 3

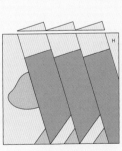

Figure 4

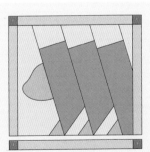

Figure 5

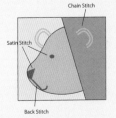

Figure 6

18

HAPPY CAT

Block Sizes

6³/₄" square or 8¹/₂" square

Templates on page 88; enlarge 250%

Fabrics and Materials

Navy print, blue solid, black solid, white solid, yellow print, and rust solid

Coordinating thread

Black embroidery floss

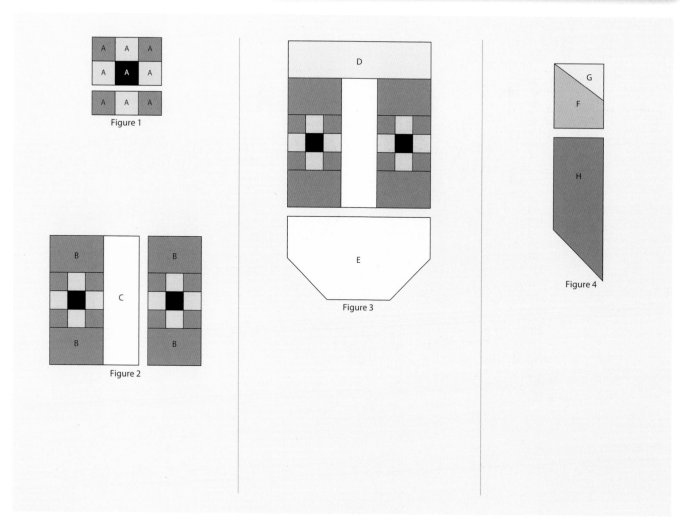

Figure 1

Figure 2

Figure 3

Figure 4

Cut the Pieces

1. From the navy print, cut eight pieces from Template A, four pieces from Template B, and one piece from Template H. Reverse Template H and cut one additional piece.

2. From the blue solid, cut eight pieces from Template A.

3. From the black solid, cut two pieces from Template A and one piece from Template J. (Note that the seam allowance for Template J is narrow. Because the shape is appliquéd, the edge is turned under at the broken line.)

4. From the white solid, cut one piece each from Templates C and E.

5. From the yellow print, cut one piece each from Templates D and G. Reverse Template G and cut one additional piece. Cut two pieces from Template I.

6. From the rust solid, cut one piece from Template F. Reverse Template F and cut one additional piece.

Assemble the Block

1. Sew the A squares together. (Figure 1) Repeat to make an additional pieced square.

2. Sew two of the B shapes to the top and bottom of one pieced square. Repeat with the remaining square. Sew these pieced shapes to the C shape. (Figure 2)

3. Sew the D and E shapes to the pieced shape. (Figure 3)

4. Sew the F, G, and H shapes together. (Figure 4) Repeat to make a reverse pieced shape.

5. Sew the pieced shapes from step 4 to the square center. (Figure 5)

6. Sew the I triangles to the square center to complete the block. (Figure 6)

7. Refer to the General Instructions for Hand Appliqué (page 8) and sew the J shape to the block. (Figure 7)

8. Refer to the General Instructions for Embroidery (page 9) and stitch the embroidered details to the block. (Figure 8)

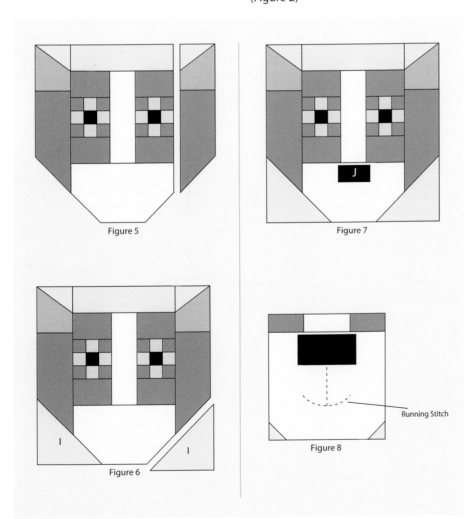

Figure 5

Figure 7

Figure 6

Figure 8

Running Stitch

HAPPY ELEPHANT

Block Sizes

7" x 5$\frac{1}{2}$" or 8$\frac{1}{2}$" x 6$\frac{3}{4}$"

Templates on page 89; enlarge 250%

Fabrics and Materials

Cream mottle, lavender print, pink print, and gold print

Coordinating thread

Orange, turquoise, and navy embroidery floss

Cut the Pieces

1. From the cream mottle, cut one piece each from Templates A, B, H, and I. Reverse Template I and cut one additional piece. Cut two pieces from Template F.

2. From the lavender print, cut one piece each from Templates C and G. (Note that the seam allowance for Template C is narrow. Because the shape is appliquéd, the edge is turned under at the broken line.) Cut two pieces from Template E. Reverse Template E and cut two additional pieces.

3. From the pink print, cut one piece from Template D. (Note that the seam allowance is narrow. Because the shape is appliquéd, the edge is turned under at the broken line.)

4. From the gold print, cut one piece from Template J.

Assemble the Block

1. Sew the A shape to the B shape. Refer to the General Instructions for Hand Appliqué (page 8) and sew the C shape to the pieced shape, and then sew the D shape to the pieced shape. (Figure 1)

2. Sew one E shape to one F shape. Trim the corner. (Figure 2)

3. Sew one E shape to the pieced shape created in step 2. (Figure 3) Repeat steps 2 and 3 to make one additional pieced shape.

4. Sew the G shape to the H shape. Sew the shapes from steps 2 and 3 to the G/H shape. (Figure 4)

5. Sew the I shapes and the J shape to the pieced shape from step 4. (Figure 5)

6. Sew the pieced shapes together to complete the block. (Figure 6)

7. Refer to the General Instructions for Embroidery (page 9) and stitch the embroidered details to the block. (Figure 7)

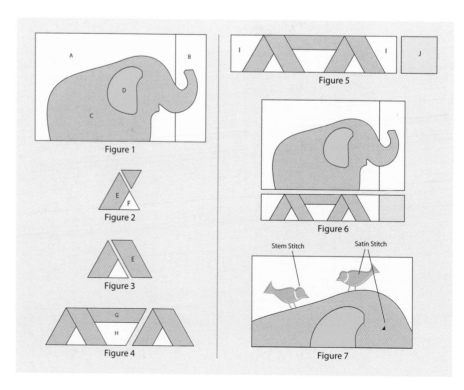

Figure 1

Figure 2

Figure 3

Figure 4

Figure 5

Figure 6

Figure 7

Stem Stitch   Satin Stitch

HAPPY MONKEY

Block Sizes

7" x 6¹/₂" or 8¹/₂" x 7³/₄"

Templates on page 90; enlarge 250%

Fabrics and Materials

Blue solid, brown solid, yellow floral, pink solid, and yellow solid

Coordinating thread

Blue and rust embroidery floss

Cut the Pieces

1. From the blue solid, cut two pieces each from Templates A, D, and F.

2. From the brown solid, cut one piece from Template B and two pieces from Template E. (Note that the seam allowance for Template E is narrow. Because the shape is appliquéd, the edge is turned under at the broken line.)

3. From the yellow floral, cut one piece from Template C and two pieces from Template D.

4. From the pink solid, cut one piece from Template G.

5. From the yellow solid, cut one piece from Template H. (Note that the seam allowance is narrow. Because the shape is appliquéd, the edge is turned under at the broken line.)

Assemble the Block

1. Refer to the General Instructions for Small Triangles (page 7) as necessary throughout and sew the A squares to the B shape. Sew the C shape to the A/B shape. (Figure 1)

2. Sew the D triangles together. (Figure 2) Repeat to make a reverse D/D shape.

3. Refer to the General Instructions for Hand Appliqué (page 8) and sew the E shape to the F shape. (Figure 3) Repeat to make a reverse E/F shape.

4. Sew the pieced shapes together. Sew the G shape to the pieced shape to complete the block. (Figure 4)

5. Refer to the General Instructions for Hand Appliqué (page 8) and sew the H shape to the block. (Figure 5)

6. Refer to the General Instructions for Embroidery (page 9) and stitch the embroidered details to the block. (Figure 6)

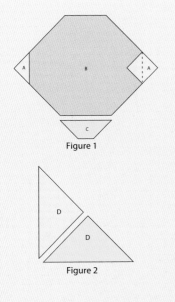

Figure 1

Figure 2

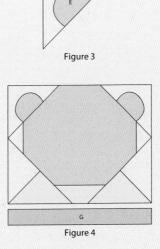

Figure 3

Figure 4

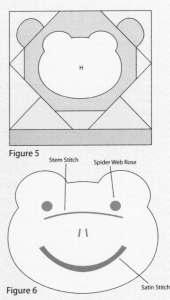

Figure 5

Figure 6

Stem Stitch

Spider Web Rose

Satin Stitch

HIPPO

Block Sizes
7" x 5^1/$_2$" or 8^1/$_2$" x 6^3/$_4$"

Templates on page 91; enlarge 250%

Fabrics and Materials
Orange print, gray solid, pink solid, and blue solid

Coordinating thread

Blue, gray, red, and white embroidery floss

Cut the Pieces

1. From the orange print, cut two pieces each from Templates A and G. Cut one piece each from Templates C, D, F, H, J, and L.

2. From the gray solid, cut one piece each from Templates B, C, E, and I. Cut three pieces from Template H and four pieces from Template K. (Note that the seam allowance for Template K is narrow. Because the shape is appliquéd, the edge is turned under at the broken line.)

3. From the pink solid, cut one piece from Template C.

4. From the blue solid, cut one piece from Template D.

Assemble the Block

1. Refer to the General Instructions for Small Triangles (page 7) as necessary throughout and sew one A square to the B shape. Sew the C shape to the A/B shape. (Figure 1)

2. Sew the D and C shapes to the pieced shape from step 1. (Figure 2)

3. Sew the D and E shapes together. Sew the pieced shapes together. (Figure 3)

4. Sew two G shapes and two gray H shapes together. Sew the G/H shape and the F shape to the pieced shape. (Figure 4)

5. Sew one A square to the I shape. (Figure 5)

6. Sew the C, remaining H, and J shapes to the pieced shape created in step 5. (Figure 6)

7. Refer to the General Instructions for Hand Appliqué (page 8) and sew the K shapes to the L shape. Sew the pieced shapes together to complete the block. (Figure 7)

9. Refer to the General Instructions for Embroidery (page 9) and stitch the embroidered details to the block. (Figure 8)

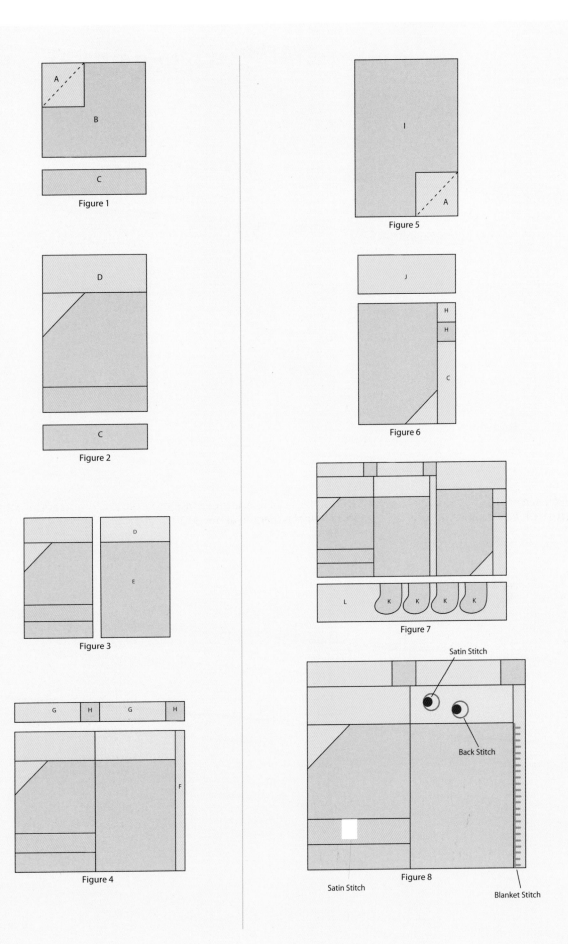

Figure 1

Figure 2

Figure 3

Figure 4

Figure 5

Figure 6

Figure 7

Figure 8

Satin Stitch

Back Stitch

Satin Stitch

Blanket Stitch

Block Sizes

8" square or 9$^1/_2$" square

Templates on page 92; enlarge 250%

Fabrics and Materials

Gold print, gray print, lavender solid, black print, burgundy print, green solid, and blue print

Coordinating thread

Purple embroidery floss

Cut the Pieces

1. From the gold print, cut one piece each from Templates A, C, F, G, J, L, M, O, Q, R, and S. Cut two pieces from Template P.

2. From the gray print, cut one piece each from Templates B, D, I, and N. Cut four pieces from Template P.

3. From the lavender solid, cut one piece each from Templates E and H.

4. From the black print, cut one K piece. (Note that the seam allowance is narrow. Because the shape is appliquéd, the edge is turned under at the broken line.)

5. From the burgundy print, cut one piece from Template P.

6. From the green solid, cut one piece from Template L.

7. From the blue print, cut two 1$^1/_8$" x 7$^1/_4$" strips and two 1$^1/_8$" x 8$^1/_2$" strips for the small block or cut two 1$^1/_4$" x 8$^1/_2$" strips and two 1$^1/_4$" x 10" strips for the large block.

Assemble the Block

1. Sew the A, B, and C shapes together. (Figure 1)

2. Sew the D, E, and F shapes together. (Figure 2)

3. Sew the G and H shapes together. (Figure 3)

4. Sew the I and J shapes together. (Figure 4)

5. Sew all the pieced shapes together. (Figure 5)

6. Refer to the General Instructions for Hand Appliqué (page 8) and sew the K shape to the L shape. (Figure 6)

7. Sew the M, N, and O shapes together. Sew the burgundy P shape to the pieced shape. Trim the ends. (Figure 7)

8. Sew the P shapes to the pieced shape and trim the ends. Repeat with the remaining P shapes, trimming the ends each time. (Figure 8)

9. Sew the Q, R, and S shapes to the pieced shape from step 8. (Figure 9)

10. Sew the pieced shapes together. (Figure 10)

11. Sew the L shape to the square center. Sew the short strips to the top and bottom and the long strips to the sides of the square center to complete the block. (Figure 11)

12. Refer to the General Instructions for Embroidery (page 9) and stitch a stem stitch along the mane and tail.

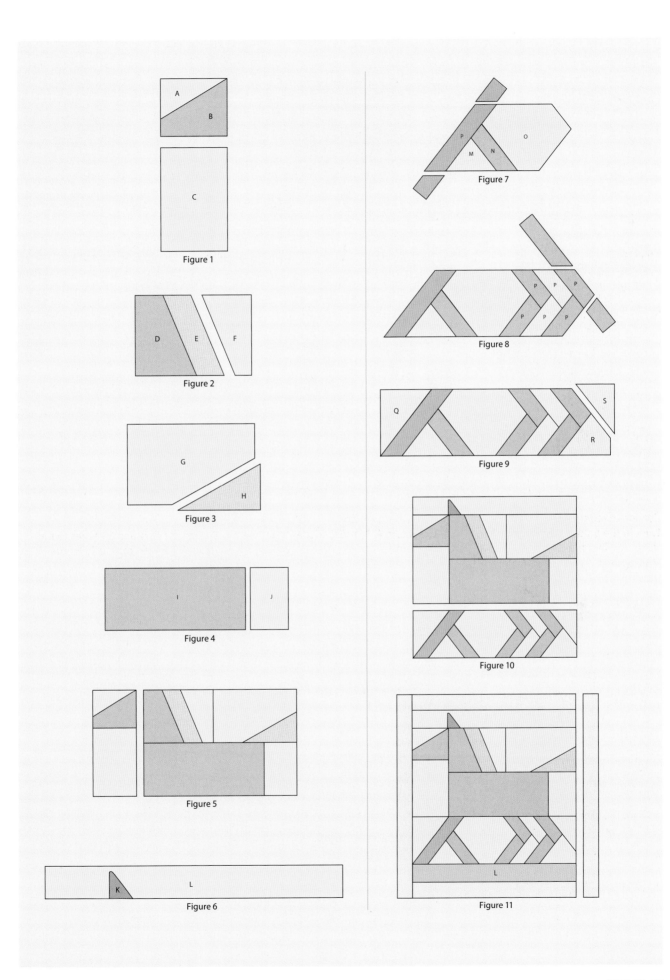

Figure 1

Figure 2

Figure 3

Figure 4

Figure 5

Figure 6

Figure 7

Figure 8

Figure 9

Figure 10

Figure 11

KANGAROO

Block Sizes

7" square or 9" square

Templates on page 93; enlarge 250%

Fabrics and Materials

Teal print, light orange print, rust solid, blue solid, medium orange print, cream solid, and dark orange print

Coordinating thread

Rust, navy, orange, and cream embroidery floss

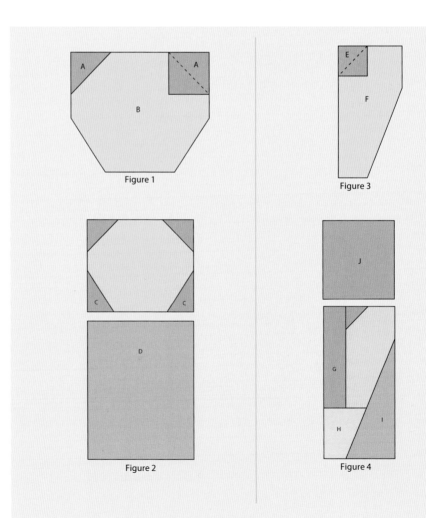

Figure 1

Figure 2

Figure 3

Figure 4

Cut the Pieces

1. From the teal print, cut two pieces each from Templates A, E, G, J, M. Cut one piece each from Templates C and L. Reverse Template C and cut one additional piece.

2. From the light orange print, cut one piece each from Templates B and F. Reverse Template F and cut one additional piece.

3. From the rust solid, cut one piece each from Templates D and I. Reverse Template I and cut one additional piece. Cut two pieces from Template K.

4. From the blue solid, cut one piece from Template H. Reverse Template H and cut one additional piece.

(Note that the seam allowance is narrow for shapes N through P. Because the shapes are appliquéd, the edge is turned under at the broken line.)

5. From the medium orange print, cut one piece from Template N.

6. From the cream solid, cut one piece from Template O.

7. From the dark orange print, cut one piece from Template P.

Assemble the Block

1. Refer to the General Instructions for Small Triangles (page 7) as necessary throughout and sew the A squares to the B shape. (Figure 1)

2. Sew the C and D shapes to the pieced shape. (Figure 2)

3. Sew the E square to the F shape. (Figure 3) Repeat to make a reverse E/F shape.

4. Sew the G shape to the E/F shape. Sew the H and I shapes to the pieced shape. Sew the J shape to the pieced shape. (Figure 4) Repeat with the reverse shape created in step 3.

5. Sew the K shapes to the L shape. (Figure 5)

6. Sew the M shapes to the pieced shape from step 5. Sew the pieced shapes together to complete the block. (Figure 6)

7. Refer to the General Instructions for Hand Appliqué (page 8) and, noting overlaps, sew the N, O, and P shapes to the block. (Figure 7)

8. Refer to the General Instructions for Embroidery (page 9) and stitch the embroidered details to the block. (Figure 8 and Figure 9)

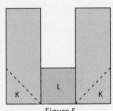

Figure 5

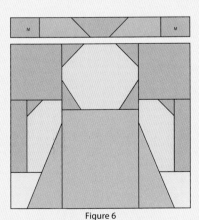

Figure 6

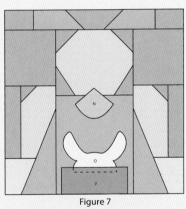

Figure 7

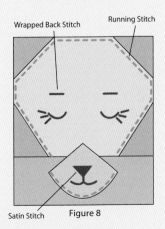

Wrapped Back Stitch   Running Stitch

Satin Stitch   Figure 8

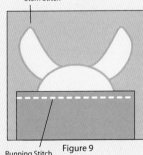

Stem Stitch

Running Stitch   Figure 9

LAMB

Block Sizes

$7^{1}/_{4}$" square or $8^{1}/_{2}$" square

Templates on page 90; enlarge 250%

Fabrics and Materials

Cream print, purple solid, lavender solid, and gray solid

Coordinating thread

Lavender and plum embroidery floss

Cut the Pieces

1. From the cream print, cut one $5^{7}/_{8}$" square for the small block or one $6^{3}/_{4}$" square for the large block.

2. From the purple solid, cut four pieces from Template A. Reverse Template A and cut four additional pieces.

3. From the lavender solid, cut one piece from Template B. (Note that the seam allowance is narrow. Because the shape is appliquéd, the edge is turned under at the broken line.)

4. From the gray solid, cut one piece from Template C. (Note that the seam allowance is narrow. Because the shape is appliquéd, the edge is turned under at the broken line.)

Assemble the Block

1. Sew four A shapes to the square. (Figure 1)

2. On the wrong side of the pieced shape, draw a square that is the reverse of the seam lines. Draw a $5^{7}/_{8}$" square for the small block or $6^{3}/_{4}$" square for the large block. (Figure 2) Trim the corners to within $^{1}/_{4}$" of the marked lines.

3. Align the edges and sew the remaining A shapes along the marked line to complete the block. (Figure 3)

4. Refer to the General Instructions for Hand Appliqué (page 8) and, noting overlaps, sew the B and C shapes to the block. (Figure 4)

5. Refer to the General Instructions for Embroidery (page 9) and stitch the embroidered details to the block. (Figure 5 or Figure 6)

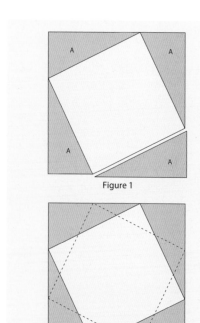

Figure 1

Figure 2

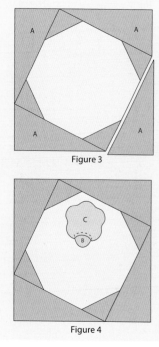

Figure 3

Figure 4

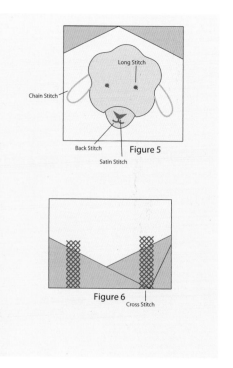

Figure 5

Figure 6

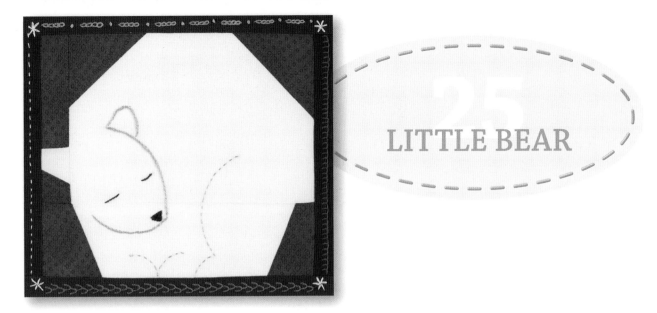

Block Sizes

7¼" x 6½" or 8½" x 7¾"

Templates on page 94; enlarge 250%

Fabrics and Materials

Blue print, white solid, and purple solid

Coordinating thread

Black, light blue, turquoise, red, green, and white embroidery floss

Cut the Pieces

1. From the blue print, cut two pieces from Template A and one piece each from Templates C, E, F, and G.

2. From the white solid, cut one piece each from Templates B, D, and G.

3. From the purple solid, cut two 1" x 6" and two 1" x 7¾" strips for the small block. Cut two 1⅛" x 6⅝" strips and two 1⅛" x 9" strips for the large block.

Assemble the Block

1. Refer to the General Instructions for Small Triangles (page 7) as necessary throughout and sew the A squares to the B shape. (Figure 1)

2. Sew the C, D, and E shapes together. (Figure 2)

3. Sew the F and G shapes together. (Figure 3)

4. Sew the pieced shapes together. (Figure 4)

5. Sew the short strips to the sides of the square center. Sew the long strips to the top and bottom of the square center to complete the block. (Figure 5)

6. Refer to the General Instructions for Embroidery (page 9) and stitch the embroidered details to the block. (Figure 6) With the red, green, turquoise, and white embroidery floss, add assorted stitches along each side of the border.

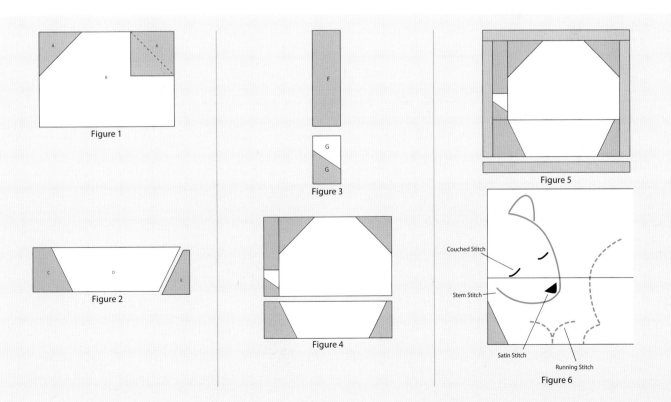

Figure 1

Figure 2

Figure 3

Figure 4

Figure 5

Couched Stitch

Stem Stitch

Satin Stitch

Running Stitch

Figure 6

26 LITTLE CHICK

Block Sizes
4³/₄" square or 6" square

Templates on page 95; enlarge 250%

Fabrics and Materials
Yellow mottle and blue print

Coordinating thread

Orange and blue embroidery floss

Cut the Pieces
1. From the yellow mottle, cut two pieces from Template A and one piece each from Templates D and G.

2. From the blue print, cut one piece each from Templates B, C, E, and H. Cut two pieces each from Templates F and I.

Assemble the Block
1. Refer to the General Instructions for Small Triangles (page 7) as necessary throughout and sew the A square to the B shape. (Figure 1)

2. Sew the C shape and the A square to the pieced shape. (Figure 2)

3. Sew the D square to the E shape. (Figure 3)

4. Sew the F squares to the G shape. (Figure 4)

5. Sew the pieced shapes together. (Figure 5)

6. Sew the H and I shapes to the square center to complete the block. (Figure 6)

7. Refer to the General Instructions for Embroidery (page 9) and stitch the embroidered details to the block. (Figure 7 and Figure 8)

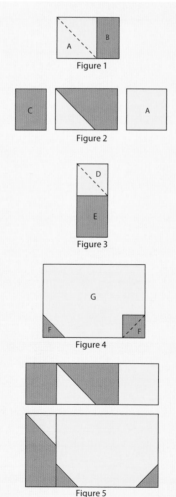

Figure 1

Figure 2

Figure 3

Figure 4

Figure 5

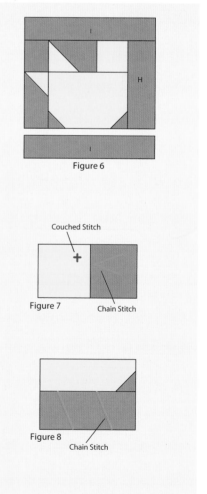

Figure 6

Couched Stitch

Figure 7

Chain Stitch

Figure 8

Chain Stitch

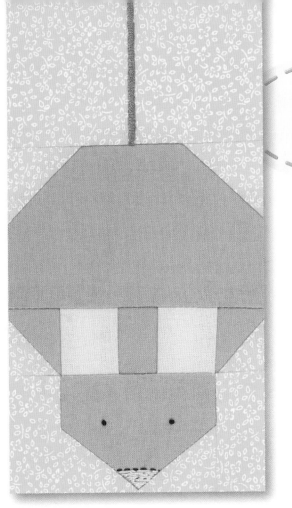

MOUSE

Block Sizes
4" x 7" or 5" x 8³/₄"

Templates on page 96; enlarge 250%

Fabrics and Materials
Yellow print, dark gray solid, and light gray solid

Coordinating thread

Navy and pink embroidery floss

Cut the Pieces
1. From the yellow print, cut one piece each from Templates A and J. Reverse Template A and cut one additional piece. Cut two pieces each from Templates C, D, and H.

2. From the dark gray solid, cut one piece each from Templates B, G, and I and two pieces from Template E.

3. From the light gray solid, cut two pieces from Template F.

Assemble the Block
1. Sew the A and B shapes together. Sew the C shapes to the pieced shape. (Figure 1)

2. Sew the E, F, and G shapes together. (Figure 2)

3. Refer to the General Instructions for Small Triangles (page 7) as necessary throughout and sew the D squares to the pieced strip created in step 2. (Figure 3)

4. Sew the H squares to the I shape. (Figure 4)

5. Sew the J shape and the pieced shapes together to complete the block. (Figure 5)

6. Refer to the General Instructions for Embroidery (page 9) and stitch the embroidered details to the block. Use satin stitch to add a tail to the block. (Figure 6)

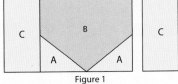

Figure 1

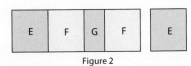
Figure 2

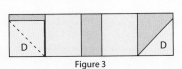
Figure 3

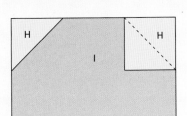
Figure 4

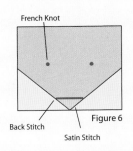
French Knot
Back Stitch
Satin Stitch
Figure 5

Figure 6

Block Sizes
6$^1/_2$" x 7" or 8$^1/_4$" x 8$^3/_4$"

Templates on page 97; enlarge 250%

Fabrics and Materials
Green solid, medium brown solid, dark brown print, light orange print, tan check, and dark orange print

Brown felt

Coordinating thread

Cream and brown embroidery floss

Cut the Pieces
1. From the green solid, cut four pieces from Template A and two pieces from Template D. Cut one piece each from Templates C, K, and L.

2. From the medium brown solid, cut two pieces from Template A and one piece each from Templates B, G, H, and J.

3. From the dark brown print, cut one piece from Template E. Reverse Template E and cut one additional piece.

4. From the light orange print, cut two pieces from Template F and one piece from Template I.

5. From the tan check, cut two pieces from Template M. (Note that the seam allowance is narrow. Because the shape is appliquéd, the edge is turned under at the broken line.)

6. From the brown felt, cut two pieces from Template N. (Note that shape N is also for Hand Appliqué, but it is cut from felt, which doesn't require a turned edge.)

7. From the dark orange print, cut one piece from Template O. (Note that the seam allowance is narrow. Because the shape is appliquéd, the edge is turned under at the broken line.)

Assemble the Block
1. Refer to the General Instructions for Small Triangles (page 7) as necessary throughout and sew one brown A square and one green A square together. (Figure 1) Make one additional A/A square.

2. Sew the A/A squares to the B shape. (Figure 2)

3. Sew the C and D shapes to the pieced shape from step 2. (Figure 3)

4. Sew one E, one F, and the G shape together. (Figure 4)

5. Sew the H, I, and J shapes together. (Figure 5)

6. Sew the reverse E and F shapes together. Sew the K and L shapes to the pieced shape from step 5. Sew the pieced shapes together. (Figure 6)

7. Sew all the pieced shapes together. Sew the remaining A squares to the pieced shape to complete the block. (Figure 7)

8. Refer to the General Instructions for Appliqué (page 8) and noting overlaps, sew the M, N, and O shapes to the block. (Figure 8)

9. Refer to the General Instructions for Embroidery (page 9) and stitch the embroidered details to the block. (Figure 9 and Figure 10)

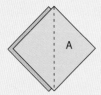

Figure 1

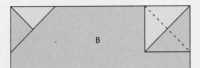

Figure 2

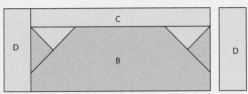

Figure 3

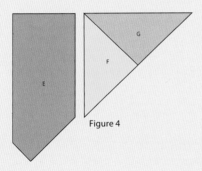

Figure 4

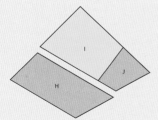

Figure 5

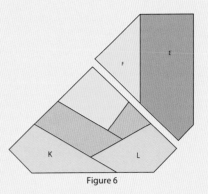

Figure 6

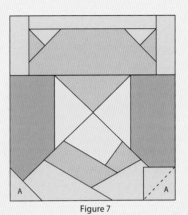

Figure 7

Figure 8

French Knot

Long Stitch

Figure 9

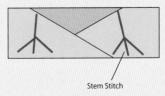

Stem Stitch

Figure 10

29 PANDA

Block Sizes

6¼" square or 7½" square

Templates on page 98; enlarge 250%

Fabrics and Materials

Yellow print, white solid, black solid, and pink solid

Coordinating thread

Light blue, gray, pink, and green embroidery floss

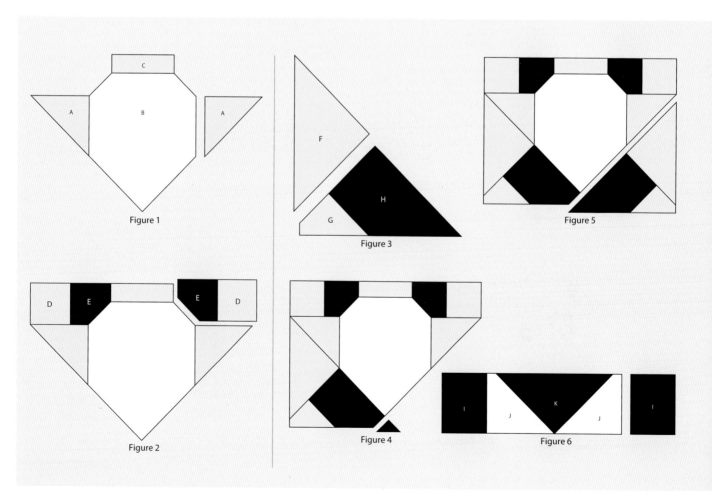

Figure 1

Figure 2

Figure 3

Figure 4

Figure 5

Figure 6

Cut the Pieces

1. From the yellow print, cut two pieces each from Templates A, D, and F. Cut one piece each from Templates C and G. Reverse Template G and cut one additional piece.

2. From the white solid, cut one piece each from Templates B and J. Reverse Template J and cut one additional piece.

3. From the black solid, cut two pieces from Templates E, I, and L. (Note that the seam allowance for Template L is narrow. Because the shape is appliquéd, the edge is turned under at the broken line.) Cut one piece each from Templates H and K. Reverse Template H and cut one additional piece.

4. From the pink solid, cut one piece from Template M. (Note that the seam allowance is narrow. Because the shape is appliquéd, the edge is turned under at the broken line.)

Assemble the Block

1. Refer to the General Instructions for Inset Seams (page 7) and starting and stopping ¹/₄" from each edge, sew the A, B, and C shapes together. (Figure 1)

2. Sew one D shape to one E shape. Repeat to make a reverse D/E shape. Starting and stopping ¹/₄" from each corner, sew the D/E shapes to the pieced shape from step 1. (Figure 2)

3. Sew one each of the F, G, and H shapes together. (Figure 3) Repeat to make a reverse pieced shape.

4. Sew one shape from step 3 to the pieced shape from step 2. Trim the corner. (Figure 4)

5. Sew the remaining shape from step 3 to the pieced shape from step 4. (Figure 5)

6. Sew the I, J, and K shapes together. (Figure 6)

7. Sew the pieced shapes together to complete the block. (Figure 7)

8. Refer to the General Instructions for Hand Appliqué (page 8) and sew the L and M shapes to the block. (Figure 8)

9. Refer to the General Instructions for Embroidery (page 9) and stitch the embroidered details to the block. (Figure 9)

Figure 7

Figure 8

Satin Stitch

Wrapped Back Stitch

Chain Stitch

Blanket Stitch   Back Stitch

Figure 9

PUPPY

Block Sizes

7" square or 8$\frac{1}{2}$" square

Templates on page 99; enlarge 250%

Fabrics and Materials

Lavender solid, blue print, gold print, and red check

Coordinating thread

Navy, brown, blue, and tan embroidery floss

Cut the Pieces

1. From the lavender solid, cut one piece each from Templates A, E, F, H, and K. Reverse Template A and cut one additional piece. Cut two pieces from Template D.

2. From the blue print, cut one piece from Template B. Reverse Template B and cut one additional piece.

3. From the gold print, cut one piece each from Templates C, G, I, and J.

4. From the red check, cut one piece from Template L. (Note that the seam allowance is narrow. Because the shape is appliquéd, the edge is turned under at the broken line.)

Assemble the Block

1. Sew the A and B shapes to the C shape. Sew the D triangles to the pieced shape. (Figure 1) Sew the reverse A, B, and D shapes to the pieced shape.

2. Sew the E shape to the pieced shape from step 1. (Figure 2)

3. Sew the F and G shapes together. (Figure 3)

4. Refer to the General Instructions for Small Triangles (page 7) as necessary throughout and sew the F/G square and the H square to the I shape. (Figure 4)

5. Sew the J square to the K shape. (Figure 5)

6. Sew the pieced shapes together to complete the block. Refer to the General Instructions for Hand Appliqué (page 8) and sew the L shape to the block. (Figure 6)

7. Refer to the General Instructions for Embroidery (page 9) and stitch the embroidered details to the block. (Figure 7 and Figure 8)

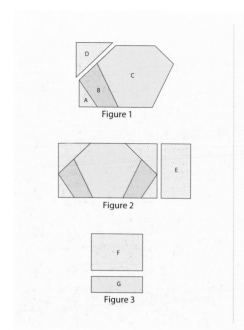

Figure 1

Figure 2

Figure 3

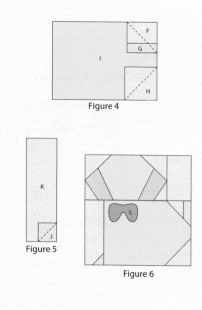

Figure 4

Figure 5

Figure 6

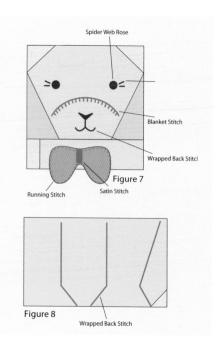

Spider Web Rose

Blanket Stitch

Wrapped Back Stitch

Figure 7

Running Stitch

Satin Stitch

Figure 8

Wrapped Back Stitch

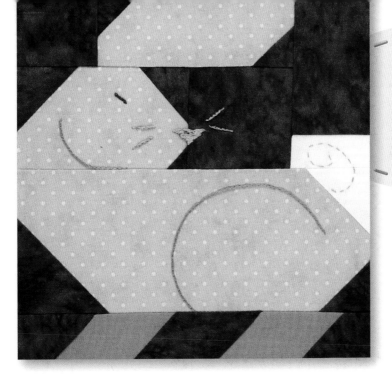

Block Sizes
6³/₄" square or 8¹/₄" square

Templates on page 100; enlarge 250%

Fabrics and Materials
Purple mottle, tan polka dot, white solid, and rust solid

Coordinating thread

Black, blue, tan, and pink embroidery floss

Cut the Pieces

1. From the purple mottle, cut one piece each from Templates A, B, C, G, H, I, K, and N. Cut three pieces from Template E and two pieces from Template M.

2. From the tan polka dot, cut one piece each from Templates D, F, and L.

3. From the white solid, cut one piece each from Templates B and J.

4. From the rust solid, cut two pieces from Template N.

Assemble the Block

1. Refer to the General Instructions for Small Triangles (page 7) as necessary throughout and sew the A, B, and C squares to the D shape. (Figure 1)

2. Sew two E squares to the F shape. (Figure 2)

3. Sew the G shape to the pieced shape from step 2. Sew the H square to the pieced shape from step 1. Sew the pieced shapes together. (Figure 3)

4. Sew the I shape to the J shape. (Figure 4)

5. Sew the B, E, and K squares to the L shape. (Figure 5)

6. Sew the M and N shapes together. Sew the pieced shapes together to complete the block. (Figure 6)

7. Refer to the General Instructions for Embroidery (page 9) and stitch the embroidered details to the block. (Figure 7 and Figure 8)

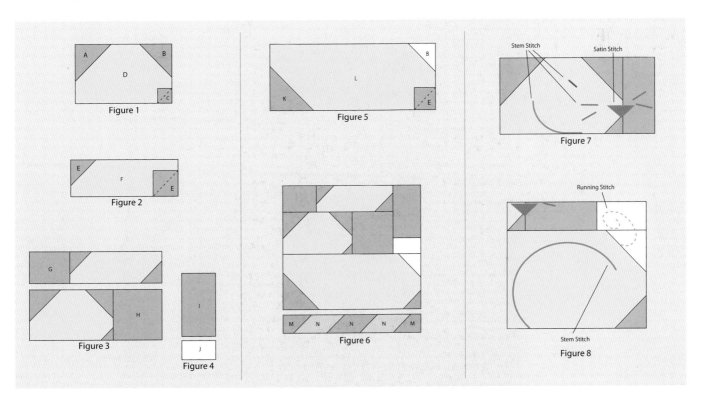

Figure 1

Figure 2

Figure 3

Figure 4

Figure 5

Figure 6

Figure 7

Figure 8

32 RACCOON

Block Sizes

8" square or 9¼" square

Templates on page 101; enlarge 250%

Fabrics and Materials

Yellow solid, rust solid, gray solid, brown solid, charcoal solid, black solid, and lavender print

Coordinating thread

Tan, brown, gray, and black embroidery floss

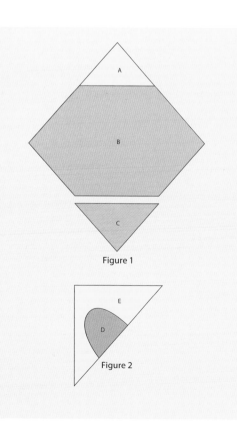

Figure 1

Figure 2

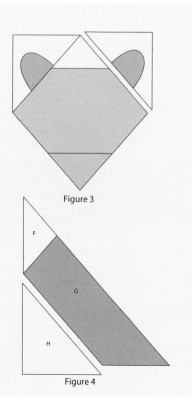

Figure 3

Figure 4

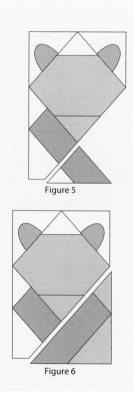

Figure 5

Figure 6

Cut the Pieces

1. From the yellow solid, cut one piece each from Templates A, I, and K. Cut one piece each from Templates E, F, and H. Reverse Template E and cut one additional piece.

2. From the rust solid, cut one piece from Template B.

3. From the gray solid, cut one piece each from Templates C and J. Cut one reverse piece each from Templates F and H.

4. From the brown solid, cut one piece from Template D. (Note that the seam allowance is narrow. Because the shape is appliquéd, the edge is turned under at the broken line.) Reverse Template D and cut one additional piece for appliqué.

5. From the charcoal solid, cut one piece from Template G. Reverse Template G and cut one additional piece.

6. From the black solid, cut two pieces from Template L. (Note that the seam allowance is narrow. Because the shapes are appliquéd, the edge is turned under at the broken line.)

7. From the lavender print, cut two 1" x 7½" and two 1" x 8½" strips for the small block or cut two 1⅛" x 8½" strips and two 1⅛" x 9¾" strips for the large block.

Assemble the Block

1. Sew the A, B, and C shapes together. (Figure 1)

2. Refer to the General Instructions for Hand Appliqué (page 8) and sew the D shape to the E shape. Repeat to make an appliquéd shape that is the reverse. (Figure 2)

3. Sew the pieced shapes together. (Figure 3)

4. Sew the yellow F and H shapes to one G shape. (Figure 4)

5. Sew the yellow and charcoal pieced shape together with the pieced shape from step 3. Trim the corner. (Figure 5)

6. Sew the gray F and H shapes to the remaining G shape. Sew the pieced shapes together. (Figure 6)

7. Sew the I and J shapes together. Refer to the General Instructions for Small Triangles (page 7) and sew the K square to the J shape. (Figure 7)

8. Sew the pieced shapes together. Sew the short strips to the sides of the square center. Sew the long strips to the top and bottom of the square center to complete the block. Refer to the General Instructions for Hand Appliqué (page 8) and sew the L shapes to the block. (Figure 8)

9. Refer to the General Instructions for Embroidery (page 9) and stitch the embroidered details to the block. (Figure 9 and Figure 10)

Figure 7

Figure 8

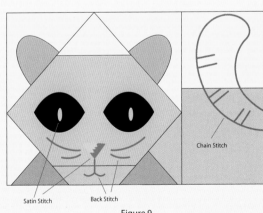

Chain Stitch

Satin Stitch   Back Stitch

Figure 9

Stem Stitch

Figure 10

SCOTTY DOG

Block Sizes
8¼" square or 10" square

Templates on page 102; enlarge 250%

Fabrics and Materials
Blue solid, black solid, lavender print, and blue floral

Gray, melon, light blue, and charcoal embroidery floss

Cut the Pieces
1. From the blue solid, cut one piece each from Templates A, B, D, E, G, I, J, K, and L.

2. From the black solid, cut one piece each from Templates A, C, G, H, and M.

3. From the lavender print, cut two pieces from Template F.

4. From the blue floral, cut four pieces from Template N.

Assemble the Block
1. Refer to the General Instructions for Small Triangles (page 7) as necessary throughout and sew the A squares together. (Figure 1)

2. Sew the B shape to the A/A square. Sew the C shape to the pieced strip. (Figure 2)

3. Sew the D shape to the pieced shape. Sew the E shape to the pieced shape. (Figure 3)

4. Sew the F shapes to the G shapes. Sew the F/G shapes to the H shape. (Figure 4)

5. Sew the I, J, and K shapes to the pieced shape. Trim the corner. (Figure 5)

6. Sew the L and M shapes together. Sew the L/M shape to the pieced shape. (Figure 6)

7. Sew the pieced shapes together. Sew the N triangles to the square center to complete the block. (Figure 7)

8. Refer to the General Instructions for Embroidery (page 9) and stitch the embroidered details to the block. Stitch a foot at the bottom of each leg. (Figure 8)

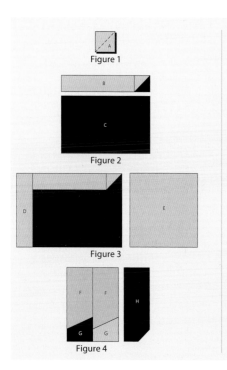

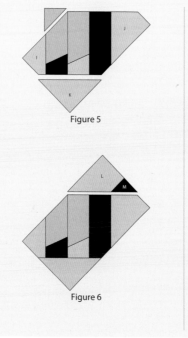

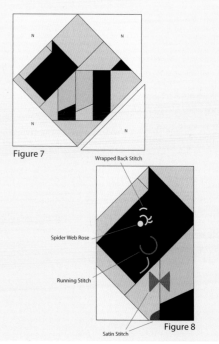

Block Sizes

7" square or 8¹/₂" square

Templates on page 103; enlarge 250%

Fabrics and Materials

Blue mottle, burgundy solid, brown solid, and tan polka dot

Coordinating thread

Light brown and dark brown embroidery floss

Cut the Pieces

1. From the blue mottle, cut one piece each from Templates A, C, D, F, H, and I.

(Note that the seam allowances for Templates L, J, and K are narrow. Because the shapes are appliquéd, the edges are turned under at the broken line.)

2. From the burgundy solid, cut one piece each from Templates B, E, G, and L.

3. From the brown solid, cut one piece from Template J.

4. From the tan polka dot, cut one piece from Template K.

Assemble the Block

1. Sew the A and B shapes together. Refer to the General Instructions for Small Triangles (page 7) and sew the C square to the A/B shape. (Figure 1)

2. Sew the D, E, and F shapes together. (Figure 2)

3. Sew the G shape to the pieced shape from step 2. (Figure 3)

4. Sew the pieced shapes together. Sew the H and I shapes to the pieced shape to complete the block. (Figure 4)

5. Refer to the General Instructions for Hand Appliqué (page 8) and sew the J, K and L shapes to the block. Unpick the seam and tuck the end of the tail in to secure; whipstitch closed. (Figure 5)

6. Refer to the General Instructions for Embroidery (page 9) and stitch the embroidered details to the block. (Figure 6)

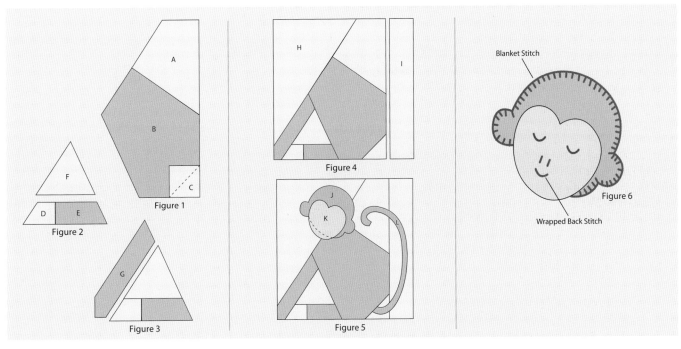

Figure 1

Figure 2

Figure 3

Figure 4

Figure 5

Figure 6

Blanket Stitch

Wrapped Back Stitch

Block Sizes
6" x 8¹/₂" and 6³/₄" x 9¹/₂"

Templates on page 104; enlarge 250%

Fabrics and Materials
Black solid, peach print, gray print, orange print, and blue print

Coordinating thread

Black and pink embroidery floss

Cut the Pieces
1. From the black solid, cut two pieces from Template A and one piece each from Templates C and H.

2. From the peach print, cut one piece each from Templates B, D, E, F, G, I, and J. Reverse Templates I and J and cut one additional piece from each.

3. From the gray print, cut one piece from Template K. (Note that the seam allowance is narrow. Because the shape is appliquéd, the edge is turned under at the broken line.)

4. From the orange print, cut two 1¹/₈" x 5¹/₄" strips and two 1¹/₈" x 7³/₄" strips for the small block or cut two 1¹/₄" x 5³/₄" strips and two 1¹/₄" x 8¹/₂" strips for the large block.

5. From the blue print, cut four pieces from Template L.

Assemble the Block
1. Sew the A triangles to the B shape. Sew the pieced shape to the C shape. (Figure 1)

2. Sew the D triangle to the pieced shape. Refer to the General Instructions for Small Triangles (page 8) and sew the E square to the pieced shape. (Figure 2)

3. Sew the F and G shapes to the pieced shape. (Figure 3)

4. Sew the I and J triangles to the H shape. (Figure 4)

5. Sew the pieced shapes together. (Figure 5)

6. Refer to the General Instructions for Hand Appliqué (page 8) and sew the K shape to the square center. (Figure 6)

7. Sew long orange print strips to the sides of the square center. Sew two L squares to one short strip. Repeat to make one additional pieced strip. Sew the pieced strips to the top and bottom of the square to complete the block. (Figure 7)

8. Refer to the General Instructions for Embroidery (page 9) and stitch the embroidered details to the block. (Figure 8)

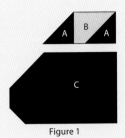

Figure 1

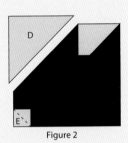

Figure 2

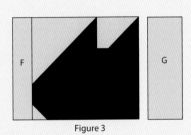

Figure 3

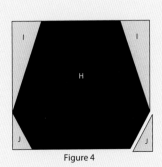

Figure 4

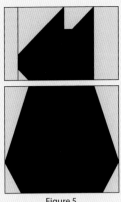

Figure 5

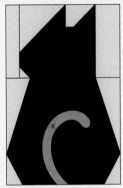

Figure 6

Figure 7

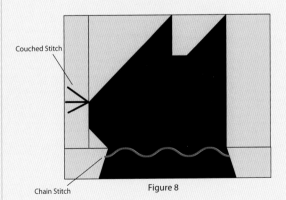

Couched Stitch

Chain Stitch

Figure 8

SNAKE

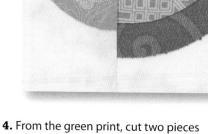

Block Sizes

6" square or 7$\frac{1}{2}$" square

Templates on page 103; enlarge 250%

Fabrics and Materials

Cream mottle, pink print, orange print, and green print

Coordinating thread

Teal and pink embroidery floss

Cut the Pieces

1. From the cream mottle, cut two pieces each from Templates A and F.

Note that the seam allowances for Templates B, C, D, E, and G are narrow. Because the shapes are appliquéd, the edges are turned under at the broken line.

2. From the pink print, cut two pieces from Template B.

3. From the orange print, cut two pieces from Template C.

4. From the green print, cut two pieces from Template D and one piece each from Templates E and G.

Assemble the Block

1. Refer to the General Instructions for Hand Appliqué (page 8) and, noting overlaps, sew one B, C, and D shape to one A square. (Figure 1) Repeat to make a second appliquéd square.

2. Sew the E shape to one F shape. (Figure 2)

3. Sew the G shape to the remaining F shape. (Figure 3)

4. Sew the appliquéd shapes together to complete the block. (Figure 4)

5. Refer to the General Instructions for Embroidery (page 9) and stitch the embroidered details to the block. (Figure 5)

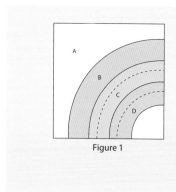

Figure 1

Figure 2

Figure 3

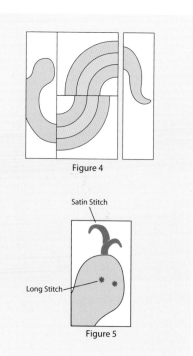

Figure 4

Figure 5

SQUIRREL

Block Sizes

6¹⁄₂" square or 8" square

Templates on page 105; enlarge 250%

Fabrics and Materials

Brown solid, pink solid, tan print, blue print, and rust solid

Coordinating thread

Brown embroidery floss

Cut the Pieces

1. From the brown solid, cut one piece each from Templates B, I, and K.

2. From the pink solid, cut two pieces from Template A and one piece each from Templates C, E, F, G, H, and J.

3. From the tan print, cut one piece each from Templates C, D, and G.

4. From the blue print, cut one piece from Template L.

5. From the rust solid, cut one piece from Template M. (Note that the seam allowance is narrow. Because the shape is appliquéd, the edge is turned under at the broken line.)

Assemble the Block

1. Refer to the General Instructions for Small Triangles (page 7) as necessary throughout and sew the A squares to the B shape. (Figure 1)

2. Sew the G shapes to the pieced shape created in step 1. (Figure 2)

3. Sew the C shapes together. Sew the D shape to the E shape. Sew the F shape to the pieced shapes. (Figure 3)

4. Sew the I square to the H shape. (Figure 4)

5. Sew the J and K shapes to the H/I shape. Sew all the pieced shapes together, and then sew the L shape to complete the block. (Figure 5)

6. Refer to the General Instructions for Hand Appliqué (page 8) and sew the M shape to the block. (Figure 6)

7. Refer to the General Instructions for Embroidery (page 9) and stitch the embroidered details to the block. (Figure 7)

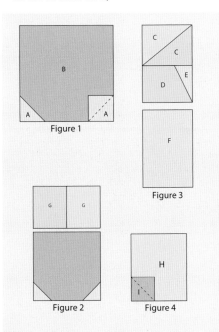

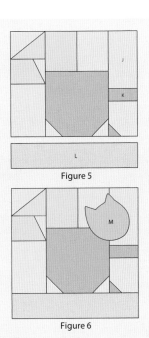

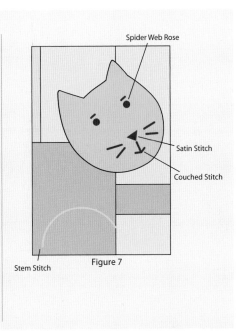

38 STAG

Block sizes

7¹/₂" square or 9" square

Templates on page 106; enlarge 250%

Fabrics and Materials

Melon solid, brown solid, white solid, blue print, purple mottle, and white print

Coordinating thread

Pink, purple, brown, blue, peach, and cream embroidery floss

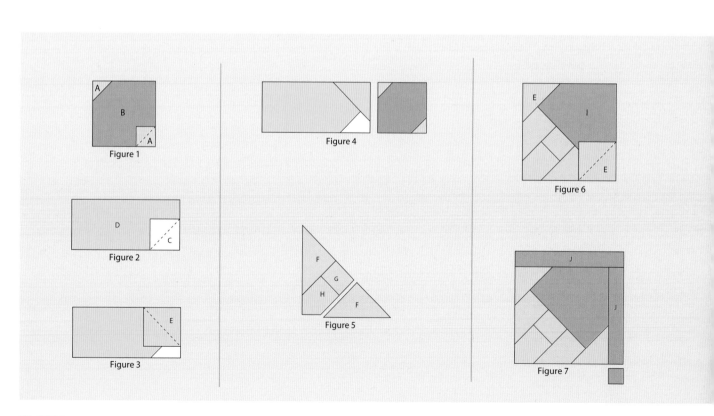

Figure 1

Figure 2

Figure 3

Figure 4

Figure 5

Figure 6

Figure 7

Cut the Pieces

1. From the melon solid, cut two pieces each from Templates A and D. Cut four pieces from Template E and one piece from Template H.

2. From the brown solid, cut one piece from Template B.

3. From the white solid, cut two pieces from Template C.

4. From the blue print, cut two pieces from Template F and one piece from Template G.

5. From the purple mottle cut two pieces from Template J and one piece from Template I.

6. From the white print, cut four pieces from Template K.

Assemble the Block

1. Refer to the General Instructions for Small Triangles (page 7) as necessary throughout and sew the A squares to the B square. (Figure 1)

2. Sew the C square to the D shape. (Figure 2) Sew one E square to the adjoining corner. (Figure 3) Repeat to make a reverse pieced shape.

3. Sew one pieced shape from step 2 to the A/B square. (Figure 4)

4. Sew the G shape to the H shape. Sew the F triangles to the G/H shape. (Figure 5)

5. Sew the I shape to the pieced shape from step 4. Sew the remaining E squares to the pieced shape. (Figure 6)

6. Sew the J strips to the pieced shape. Trim the end. (Figure 7)

7. Sew all the pieced shapes together. (Figure 8)

8. Sew the K triangles to the square center to complete the block. (Figure 9)

9. Refer to the General Instructions for Embroidery (page 9) and stitch the embroidered details to the block. (Figure 10)

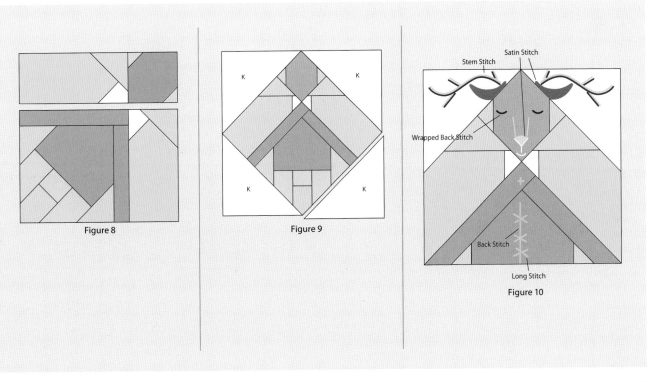

Figure 8

Figure 9

Figure 10

STANDING CAT

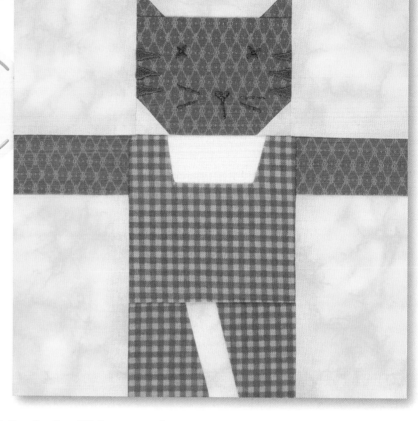

Block sizes
7" square and 8¹/₂" square

Templates on page 105; enlarge 250%

Fabrics and Materials
Orange print, yellow mottle, white solid, and blue check

Coordinating thread

Brown and navy embroidery floss

Cut the Pieces
1. From the orange print, cut two pieces each from Templates A and I. Cut one piece from Template C.

2. From the yellow mottle, cut two pieces each from Templates A, D, and J. Cut one piece each from Templates B and H.

3. From the white solid, cut one piece from Template E. (Note that the seam allowance is narrow. Because the shape is appliquéd, the edge is turned under at the broken line.)

4. From the blue check, cut one piece from Template F and two pieces from Template G.

Assemble the Block
1. Refer to the General Instructions for Small Triangles (page 7) as necessary throughout and sew the orange A squares to the B shape. (Figure 1)

2. Sew the yellow A squares to the C shape. (Figure 2)

3. Sew the pieced shapes together. Sew the D shapes to the pieced shape. (Figure 3)

4. Refer to the General Instructions for Hand Appliqué (page 8) and sew the E shape to the F shape. (Figure 4)

5. Sew the G and H shapes together. (Figure 5)

6. Sew the I shapes to the J shapes. Sew the I/J shapes to the pieced shape. (Figure 6)

7. Sew the pieced shapes together to complete the block. (Figure 7)

8. Refer to the General Instructions for Embroidery (page 9) and stitch the embroidered details to the block. (Figure 8)

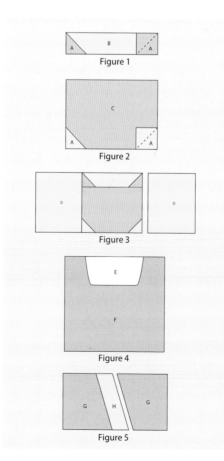

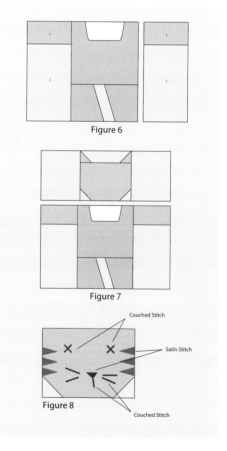

Block sizes

7" square or 8½" square

Templates on page 96; enlarge 250%

Fabrics and Materials

Cream print, white solid, multi stripe, burgundy solid, and black solid

Coordinating thread

Charcoal and white embroidery thread

Cut the Pieces

1. From the cream print, cut one piece each from Templates A, C, D, and H. Reverse Templates C and D and cut one additional piece from each. Cut two pieces from Template J.

2. From the white solid, cut one piece from Template B.

3. From the multi stripe, cut one piece from Template E and two pieces from Template I.

4. From the burgundy solid, cut one piece from Template F and two pieces from Template G.

5. From the black solid, cut one piece each from Templates K and L. Reverse Template L and cut one additional piece. (Note that the seam allowances for Templates K and L are narrow. Because the shapes are appliquéd, the edges are turned under at the broken line.)

Assemble the Block

1. Sew the A and B shapes together. Sew the C triangles to the A/B shape. (Figure 1)

2. Sew the D shapes to the pieced shape. (Figure 2)

3. Sew the G and H shapes together. Sew the E and F shapes to the G/H shape. (Figure 3)

4. Sew the I and J shapes together. Sew the I/J shapes to the pieced shape from step 3 . (Figure 4)

5. Sew the pieced shapes together to complete the block. Refer to the General Instructions for Hand Appliqué (page 8) and sew the K and L shapes to the block. (Figure 5)

6. Refer to the General Instructions for Embroidery (page 9) and stitch the embroidered details to the block. (Figure 6)

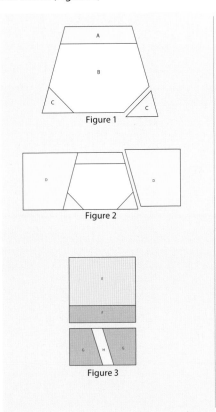

Figure 1

Figure 2

Figure 3

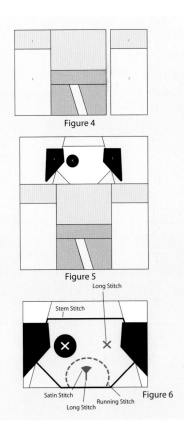

Figure 4

Figure 5

Figure 6

Long Stitch

Stem Stitch

Satin Stitch

Running Stitch

Long Stitch

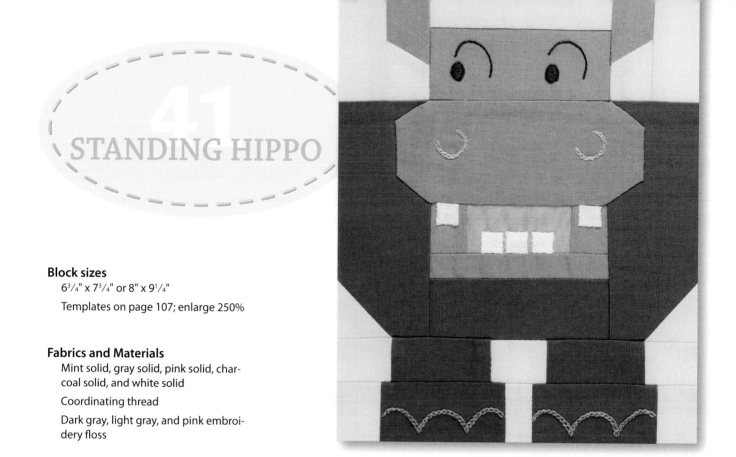

STANDING HIPPO

41

Block sizes

6³/₄" x 7³/₄" or 8" x 9¹/₄"

Templates on page 107; enlarge 250%

Fabrics and Materials

Mint solid, gray solid, pink solid, charcoal solid, and white solid

Coordinating thread

Dark gray, light gray, and pink embroidery floss

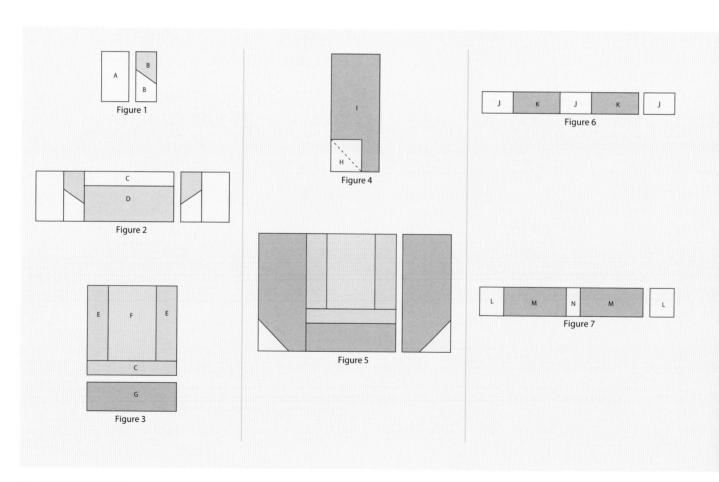

Figure 1

Figure 2

Figure 3

Figure 4

Figure 5

Figure 6

Figure 7

Cut the Pieces

1. From the mint solid, cut two pieces each from Templates A, H, and L. Cut one piece each from Templates B, C and N. Reverse Template B and cut one additional piece. Cut three pieces from Template J.

2. From the gray solid, cut one piece from Template B. Reverse Template B and cut one additional piece. Cut one piece each from Templates D, E, C and O. (Note that the seam allowance for Template O is narrow. Because the shape is appliquéd, the edge is turned under at the broken line.)

3. From the pink solid, cut one piece from Template F.

4. From the charcoal solid, cut one piece from Template G, and two pieces each from Templates I, K, and M.

5. From the white solid, cut five P pieces. (Note that the seam allowance is narrow. Because the shape is appliquéd, the edge is turned under at the broken line.)

Assemble the Block

1. Sew the A shape to the B shapes. (Figure 1) Repeat to make a reverse A/B shape.

2. Sew the mint C and the D shapes to the A/B shapes. (Figure 2)

3. Sew the gray C and E shapes to the F shape. Sew the G shape to the pieced shape. (Figure 3)

4. Refer to the General Instructions for Small Triangles (page 7) and sew one H square to the I shape. Repeat to make a reverse H/I shape. (Figure 4)

5. Sew the pieced shapes from steps 3 and 4 together. (Figure 5)

6. Sew the J and K shapes together. (Figure 6)

7. Sew the L, M, and N shapes together. (Figure 7)

8. Sew the pieced shapes together to complete the block. (Figure 8)

9. Refer to the General Instructions for Hand Appliqué (page 8) and sew the O and P shapes to the block. (Figure 9) Machine zigzag along the edges of the P shapes.

10. Refer to the General Instructions for Embroidery (page 9) and stitch the embroidered details to the block. (Figure 10 and Figure 11)

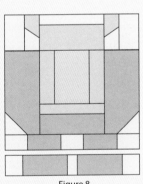

Figure 8

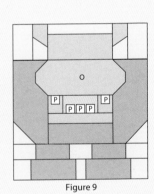

Figure 9

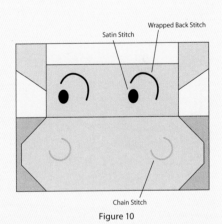

Figure 10

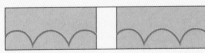

Figure 11

STANDING LION

Block sizes

7" square and 8$\frac{1}{2}$" square

Templates on page 108; enlarge 250%

Fabrics and Materials

Purple mottle, gold print, rust solid, white solid, and multi print

Coordinating thread

Brown and mauve embroidery floss

Cut the Pieces

1. From the purple mottle, cut four pieces from Template A.

2. From the gold print, cut two pieces from Template A. Cut one piece each from Templates B, D, J, and H, and cut four pieces from Template E.

3. From the rust solid, cut ten pieces from Template A.

4. From the white solid, cut two pieces each from Templates A, E, I, and H. Cut one piece each from Templates D, C, F, G, and K.

5. From the multi print, cut two pieces from Template A.

Assemble the Block

1. Refer to the General Instructions for Small Triangles (page 7) as necessary throughout and sew the purple A squares to the B shape. (Figure 1)

2. Sew two rust A squares to the C shape. (Figure 2)

3. Sew two rust A squares to the D shape. (Figure 3)

4. Sew two gold E shapes to the F shape. Trim the ends. Sew the pieced shapes together. (Figure 4)

5. Sew one rust and one white A square together to make a pieced square. (Figure 5) Make one additional rust/white square. Make two rust/gold squares.

6. Sew two rust A squares to the G shape. (Figure 6)

7. Sew one rust/white square to the shape from step 6. Sew the H and I shapes to the pieced shape. (Figure 7)

8. Sew the remaining A/A squares together. Sew the H squares to the pieced shape. (Figure 8)

9. Sew the multi A squares to the J shape. (Figure 9)

10. Sew the K shape to the pieced shape from step 9. Sew this pieced shape to the shape from step 8. Sew the gold and white E shapes to the I shape. Sew the pieced shapes together. Trim the end. (Figure 10)

11. Sew the pieced shapes together to complete the block. (Figure 11)

12. Refer to the General Instructions for Embroidery (page 9) and stitch the embroidered details to the block. (Figure 12)

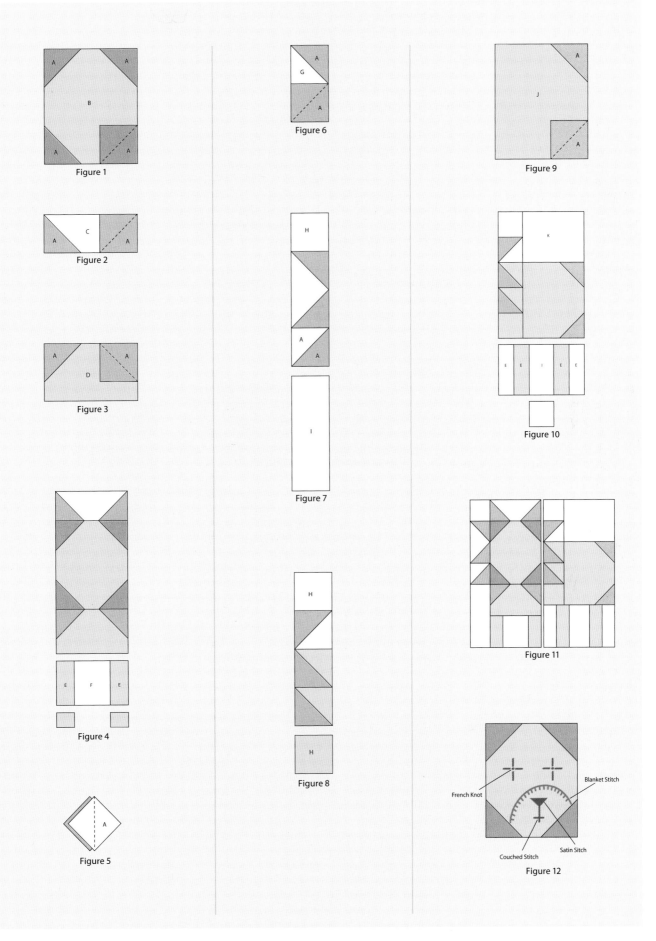

Figure 1

Figure 2

Figure 3

Figure 4

Figure 5

Figure 6

Figure 7

Figure 8

Figure 9

Figure 10

Figure 11

French Knot
Blanket Stitch
Couched Stitch
Satin Sitch

Figure 12

43 TIGER

Block sizes

5½" x 9" or 6½" x 10"

Templates on page 109; enlarge 250%

Fabrics and Materials

Orange solid, orange print, brown print, and yellow solid

Coordinating thread

Tan, brown, and cream embroidery floss

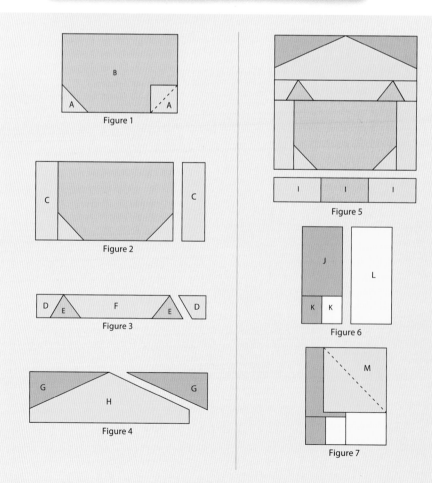

Figure 1

Figure 2

Figure 3

Figure 4

Figure 5

Figure 6

Figure 7

Cut the Pieces

1. From the orange solid, cut one piece each from Templates B, E, and I. Reverse Template E and cut one additional piece.

2. From the orange print, cut two pieces each from Templates A, C, I, and M. Cut one piece each from Templates D, F, H, and L. Reverse Template D and cut one additional piece.

3. From the brown print, cut one piece each from Templates G, J, L, N, P, Q, and R. Reverse Template G and cut one additional piece. Cut two pieces from Template K.

4. From the yellow solid, cut two pieces from Template K and one piece each from Templates L and O.

Assemble the Block

1. Refer to the General Instructions for Small Triangles (page 7) as necessary throughout and sew the A squares to the B shape. (Figure 1)

2. Sew the C shapes to the A/B shape. (Figure 2)

3. Sew the D, E, and F shapes together. (Figure 3)

4. Sew the G and H shapes together. (Figure 4)

5. Sew the pieced shapes together. Sew the I shapes together, and then sew the I/I/I strip to the pieced shape. (Figure 5)

6. Sew one brown and one yellow K shape together. Sew the J and yellow L shapes to the K/K shape. (Figure 6)

7. Sew one M square to the pieced shape. (Figure 7)

8. Sew the remaining L shapes together. Sew the remaining M square to the L/L shape. (Figure 8)

9. Sew the remaining two K shapes together. Sew the N and O shapes to the K/K shape. (Figure 9)

10. Sew the P and Q shapes to the pieced shape from step 9. (Figure 10)

11. Sew the R shape to the pieced shapes to complete the block. (Figure 11)

12. Refer to the General Instructions for Embroidery (page 9) and stitch the embroidered details to the block. (Figures 12, 13, and 14) With the brown floss, use the Satin Stitch to stitch random stripes.

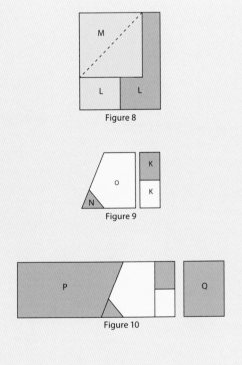

Figure 8

Figure 9

Figure 10

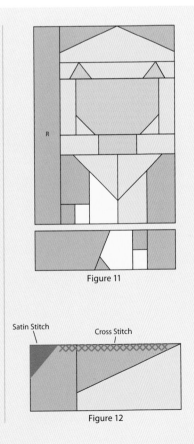

Figure 11

Figure 12

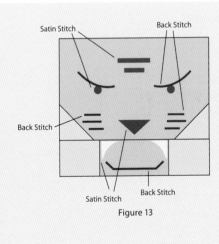

Figure 13

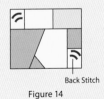

Figure 14

Block sizes

7" square or 8³/₄" square

Templates on page 110; enlarge 250%

Fabrics and Materials

Blue check, pink solid, blue solid, and pink print

Coordinating thread

Navy and pink embroidery floss

Cut the Pieces

1. From the blue check, cut one piece each from Templates B, D, E, H, and I. Cut two pieces from Template J. (Note that the seam allowance for Template J is narrow. Because the shape is appliquéd, the edge is turned under at the broken line.)

2. From the pink solid, cut one piece each from Templates A, D, E, F, H, I, and G. Reverse Template A and cut one additional piece.

3. From the blue solid, cut one piece from the C Template.

4. From the pink print, cut one piece from the K Template.

Assemble the Block

1. Sew the A triangles to the B shape. (Figure 1)

2. Sew the D and C shapes together. (Figure 2)

3. On the wrong side of the pieced shape created in step 2, draw the curve from the B shape. (Figure 3)

4. Refer to the General Instructions for Curved Patch Piecing (page 8) and sew the pieced shapes together. (Figure 4)

5. Sew the E and F shapes together. (Figure 5)

6. Refer to the General Instructions for Small Triangles (page 7) and sew the I squares to the H shapes. (Figure 6)

7. Sew the pieced shapes from steps 5 and 6 together. Then sew the G shape to the pieced shape. (Figure 7)

8. Refer to the General Instructions for Hand Appliqué (page 8) and sew the J shapes to the K shape. (Figure 8)

9. Sew the pieced shapes together to complete the block. (Figure 9)

10. Refer to the General Instructions for Embroidery (page 9) and add the stitched details. (Figure 10 and Figure 11)

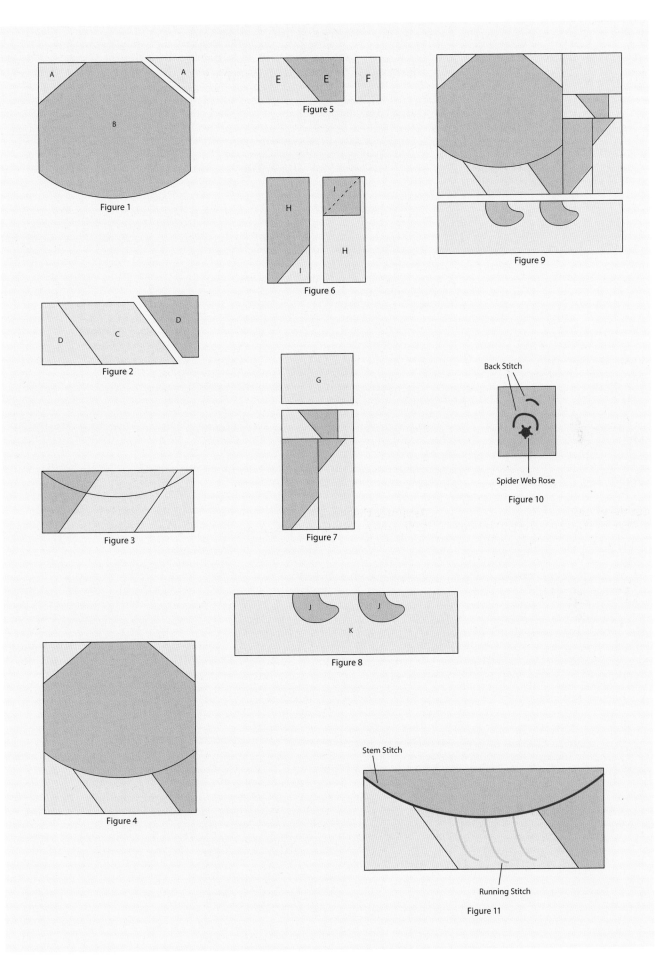

Figure 1

Figure 2

Figure 3

Figure 4

Figure 5

Figure 6

Figure 7

Figure 8

Figure 9

Figure 10

Back Stitch

Spider Web Rose

Figure 11

Stem Stitch

Running Stitch

45
WHITE RABBIT

Block sizes
7" square or 8½" square

Templates on page 111; enlarge 250%

Fabrics and Materials
Cream print, purple solid, gold print, and blue solid

Coordinating thread

Pink, navy, and turquoise embroidery floss

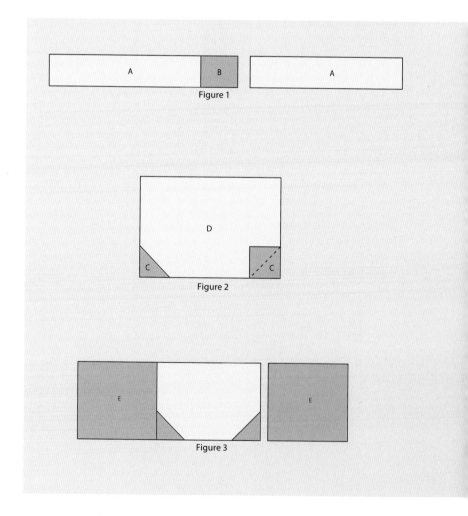

Figure 1

Figure 2

Figure 3

Cut the Pieces

1. From the cream print, cut two pieces from Template A and one piece from Template D.

2. From the purple solid, cut one piece from Templates B and I. Cut two pieces each from Templates C, E, and K.

3. From the gold print, cut one piece from Template F. (Note that the seam allowance is narrow. Because the shape is appliquéd, the edge is turned under at the broken line.)

4. From the blue solid, cut one piece from Template G and two pieces each from Templates H and J.

Assemble the Block

1. Sew the A and B shapes together. (Figure 1)

2. Refer to the General Instructions for Small Triangles (page 7) as necessary throughout and sew the C squares to the D shape. (Figure 2)

3. Sew the E shapes to the pieced shape from step 2. (Figure 3)

4. Refer to the General Instructions for Hand Appliqué (page 8) and sew the F shape to the G shape. (Figure 4)

5. Sew the H and I shapes together. (Figure 5)

6. Sew the J and K shapes together. Sew the pieced shapes together to complete the block. (Figure 6 and Figure 7)

7. Refer to the General Instructions for Embroidery (page 9) and stitch the embroidered details to the block. (Figure 8)

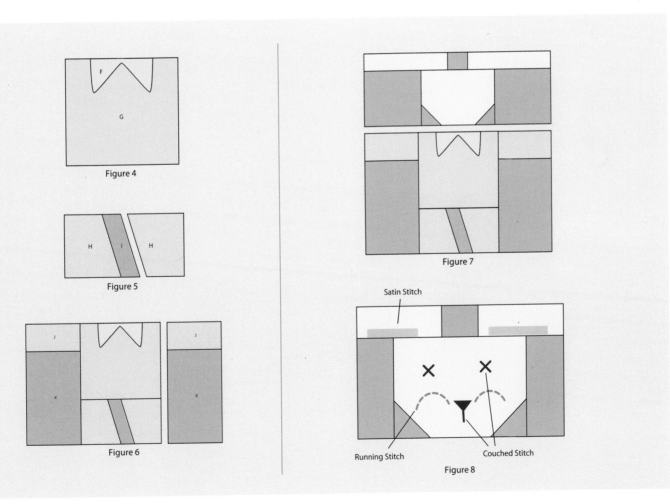

Figure 4

Figure 5

Figure 6

Figure 7

Satin Stitch

Running Stitch

Couched Stitch

Figure 8

1
BABY ELEPHANT

6³/₄" x 6"

8¹/₂" x 7¹/₂"

shading indicates area
included in seam

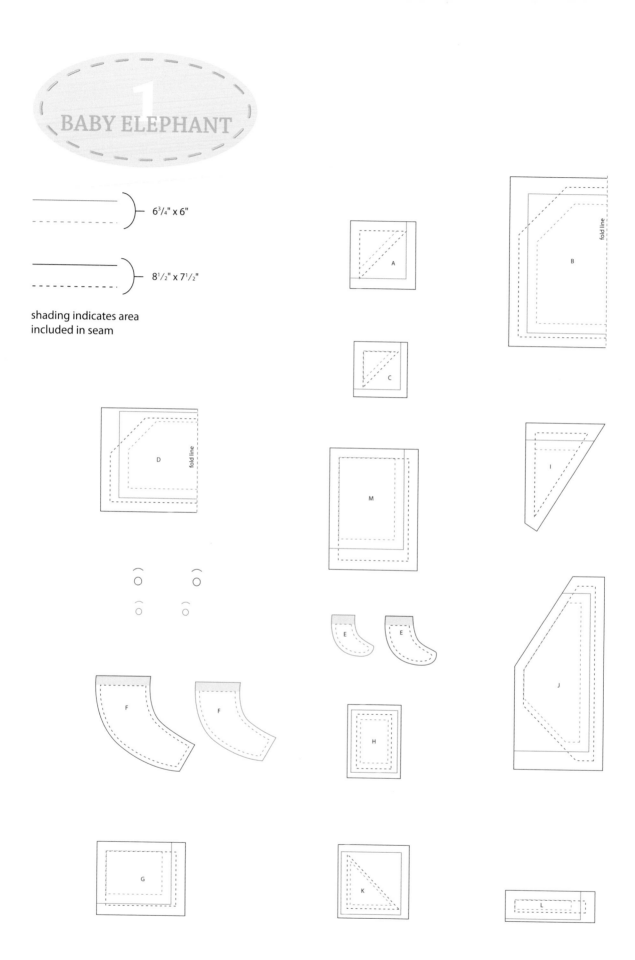

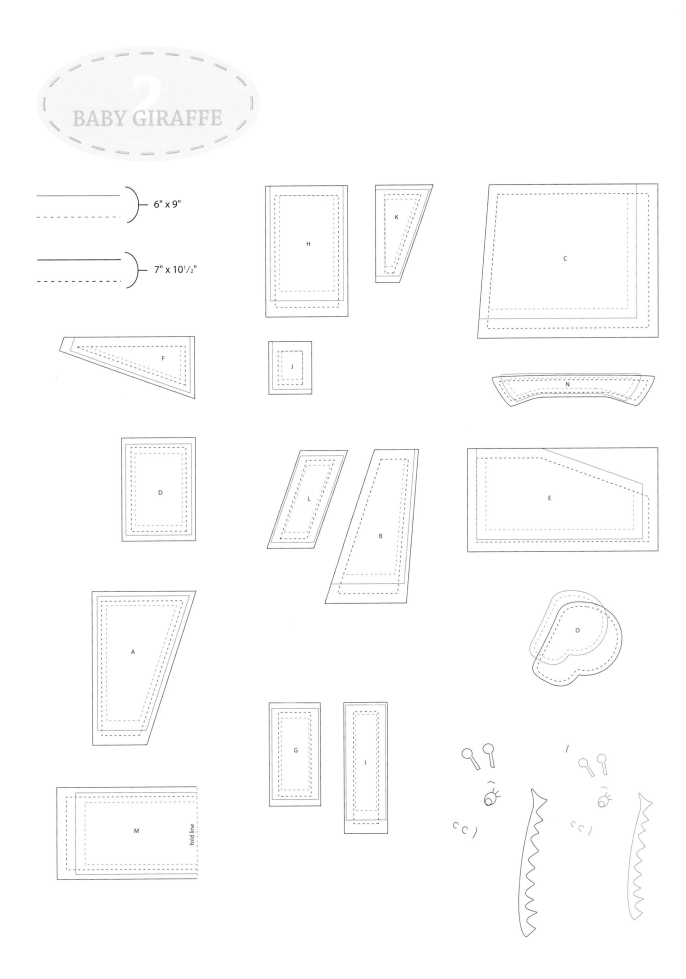

2

BABY GIRAFFE

6" x 9"

7" x 10½"

H

K

C

F

J

N

D

L

B

E

A

O

G

I

M

fold line

3
BLUEBIRD

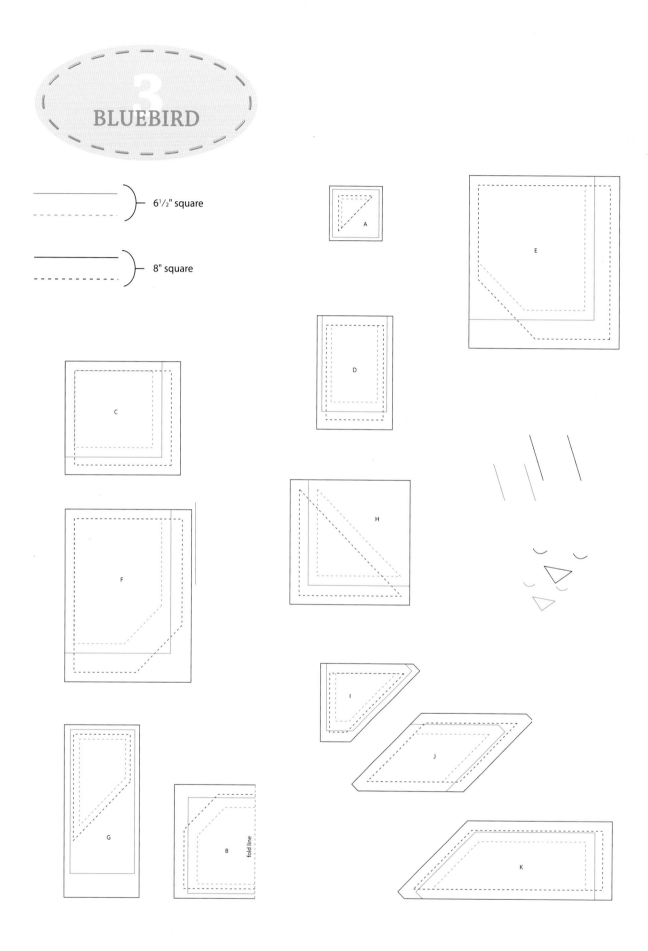

——— 6½" square

- - - - 8" square

A

E

D

C

F

H

I

J

G

B

fold line

K

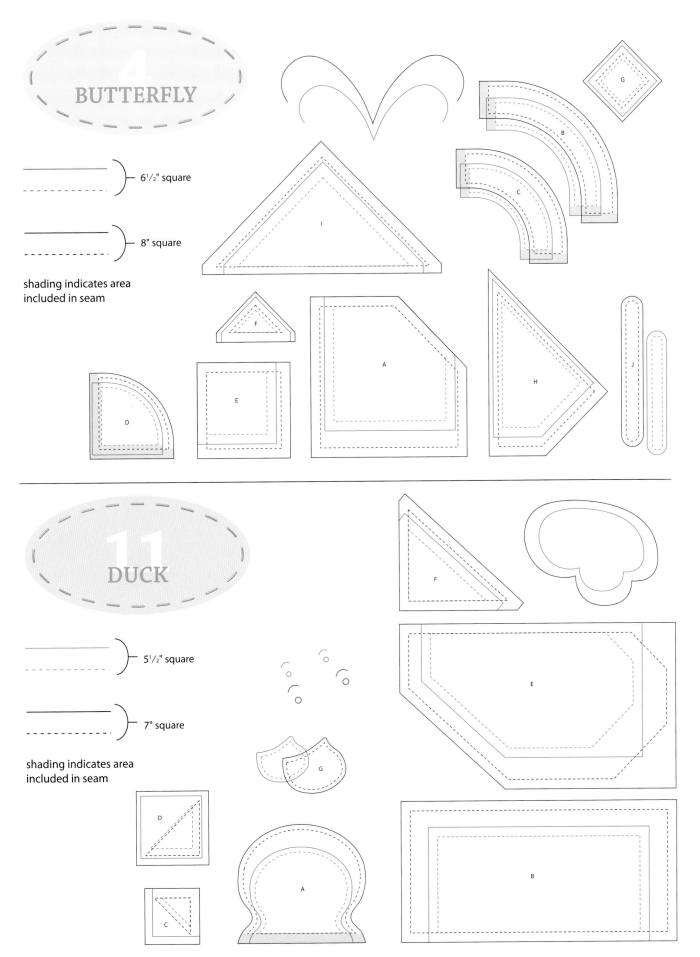

4 BUTTERFLY

——— 6 1/2" square

- - - - 8" square

shading indicates area
included in seam

11 DUCK

——— 5 1/2" square

- - - - 7" square

shading indicates area
included in seam

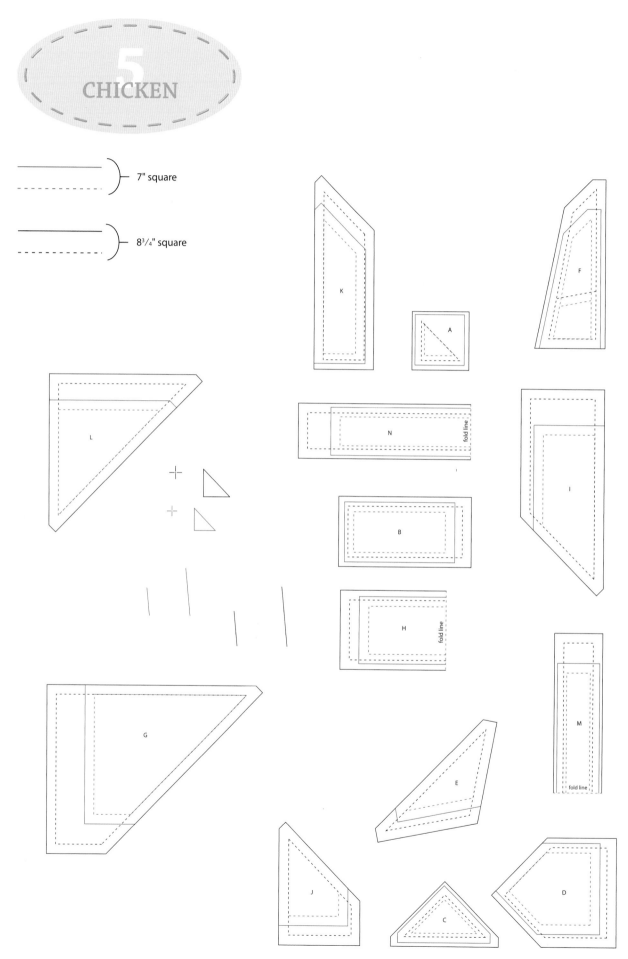

5
CHICKEN

7" square

8³/₄" square

K

A

F

L

N   fold line

B

I

H   fold line

M   fold line

G

E

J

C

D

CIRCUS ELPHANT

6

6¹/₂" square

8¹/₂" square

K

E

I

A

C

G

B

F

L

J

H

D

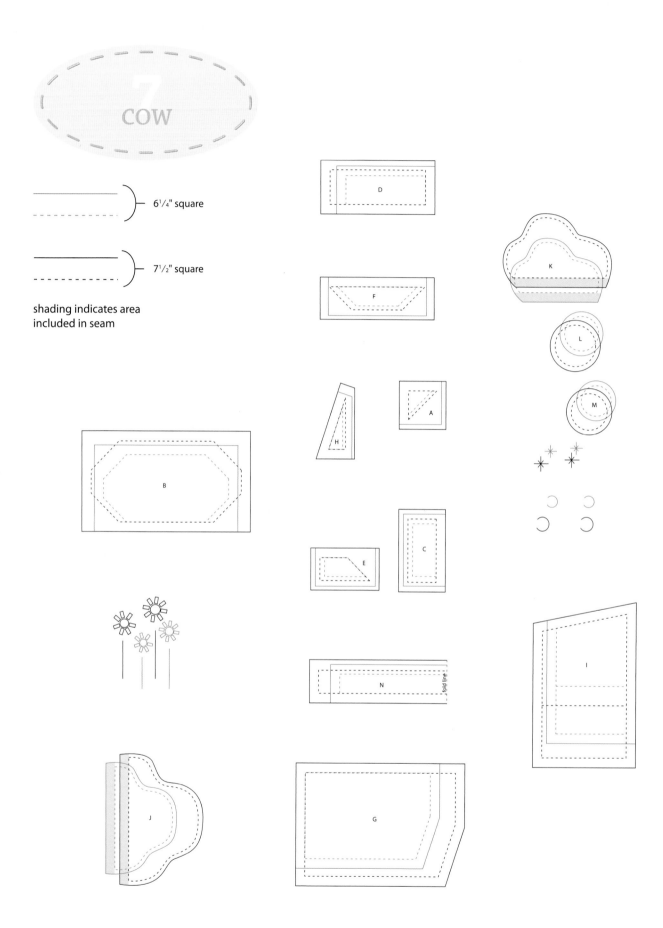

7
COW

6¼" square

7½" square

shading indicates area
included in seam

D

F

K

L

M

B

H

A

E

C

I

N

fold line

J

G

CROCODILE

8

7" x 6¼"

8½" x 7½"

shading indicates area
included in seam

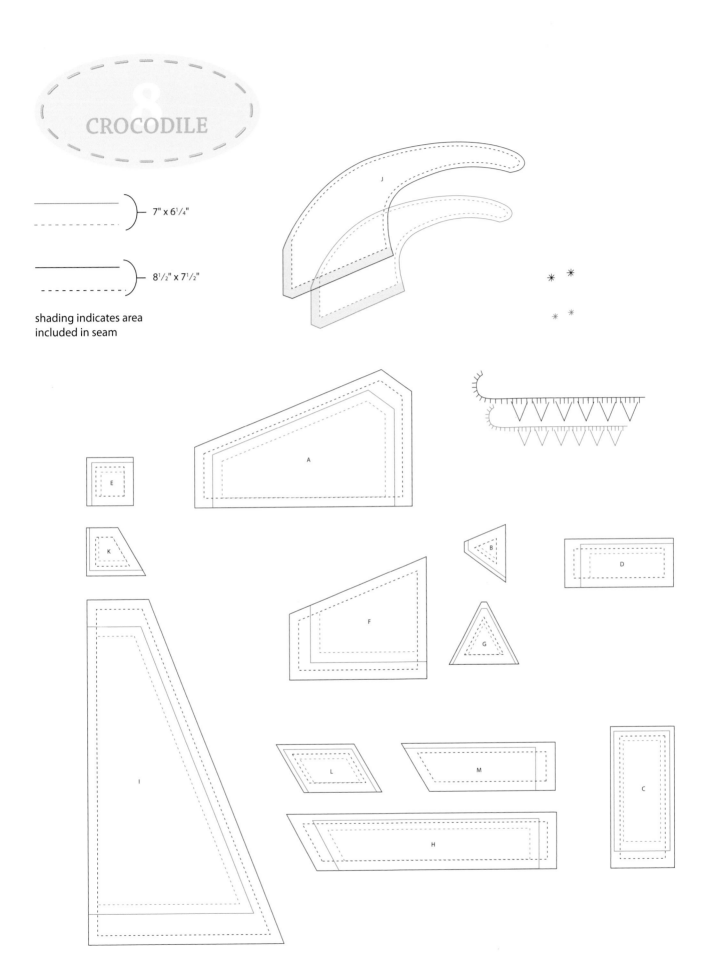

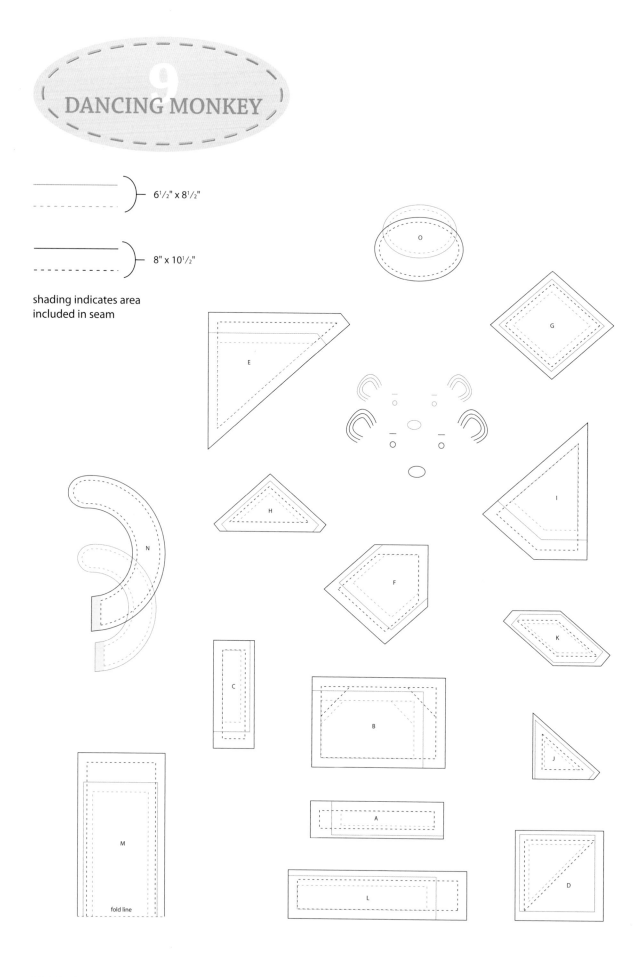

9
DANCING MONKEY

6¹⁄₂" x 8¹⁄₂"

8" x 10¹⁄₂"

shading indicates area
included in seam

O

G

E

N

H

I

F

K

C

B

J

M

A

L

D

fold line

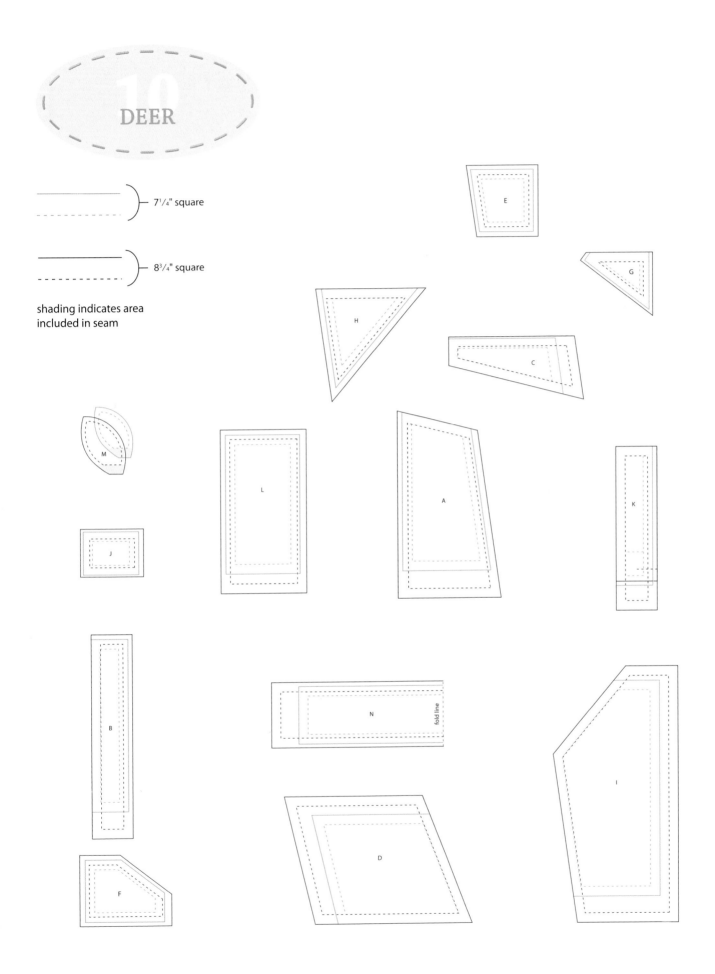

DEER

7¹/₄" square

8³/₄" square

shading indicates area
included in seam

E

G

H

C

M

L

A

K

J

B

N

fold line

I

F

D

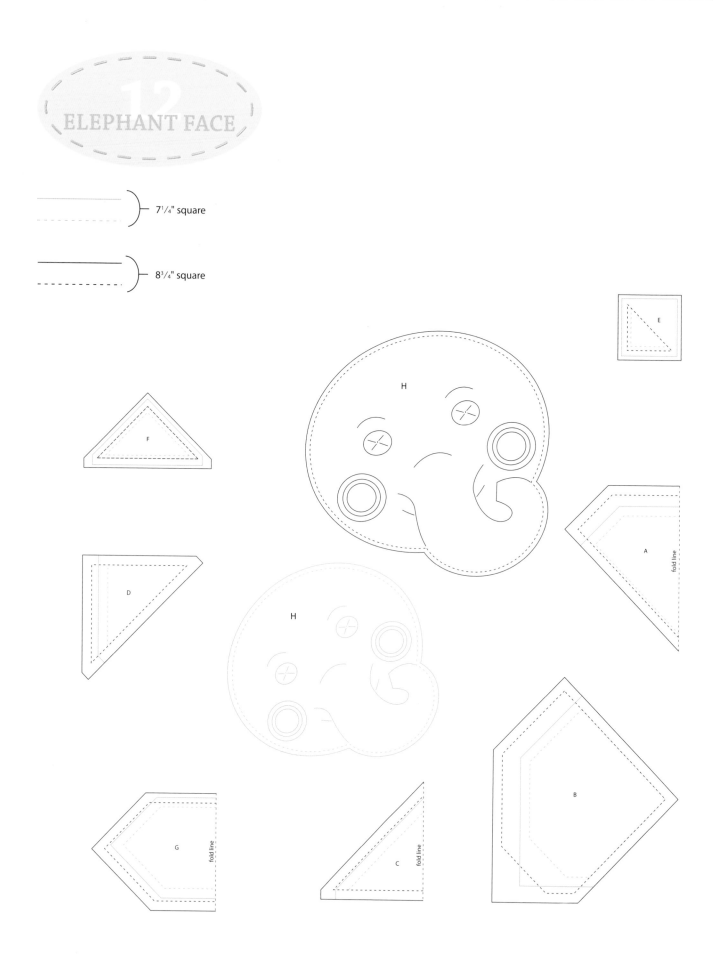

12 ELEPHANT FACE

7¼" square

8¾" square

E

F

H

A   fold line

D

H

B

G   fold line

C   fold line

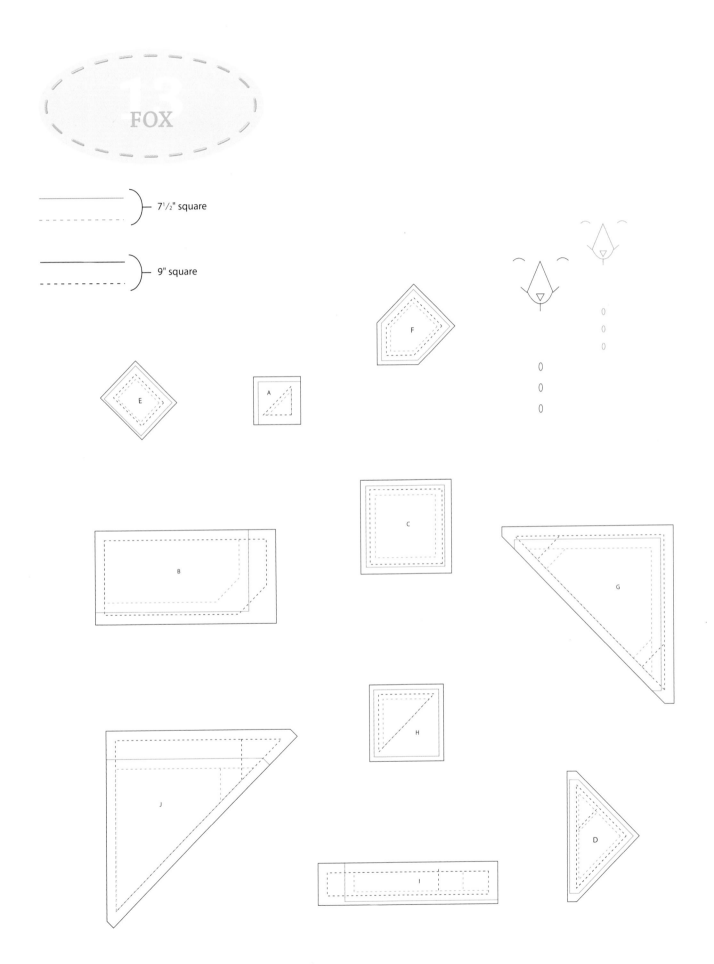

FOX

7½" square

9" square

F

E   A

C   G
B

H

J   D

I

14
FROG

6¼" square

7½" square

J

C

F

I

H

G

K

D

A

E

B

fold line

15
GECKO

—— 6" x 7¼"

—— 7½" x 9"

H

L

K

D   fold line

A

C

F

I

B

J

G

E

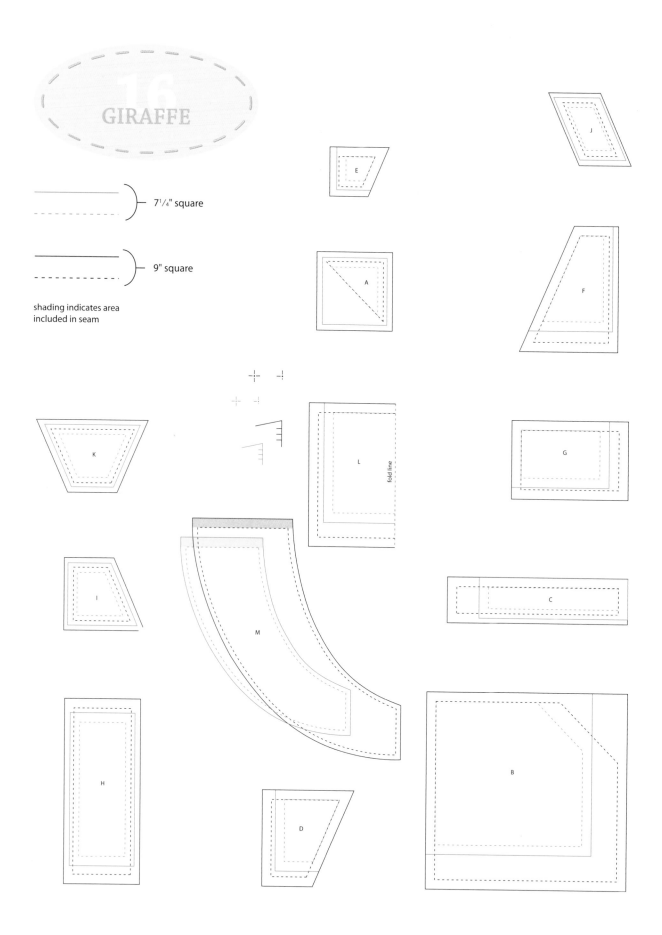

16
GIRAFFE

7¼" square

9" square

shading indicates area
included in seam

J

E

A

F

K

L

fold line

G

I

M

C

H

D

B

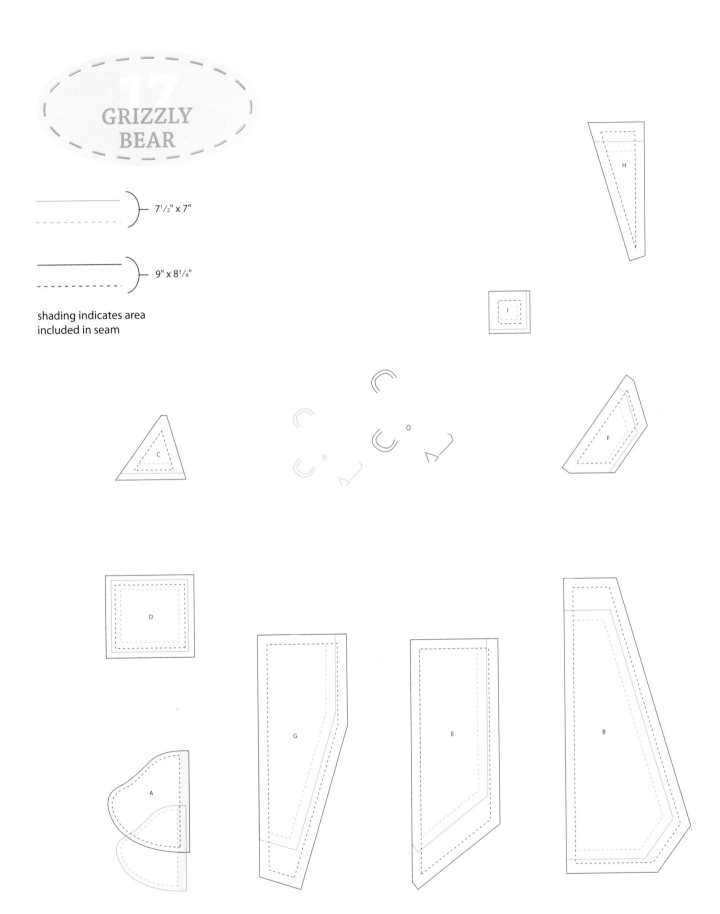

GRIZZLY BEAR

17

7½" x 7"

9" x 8³⁄₈"

shading indicates area
included in seam

H

I

C

F

D

G

E

B

A

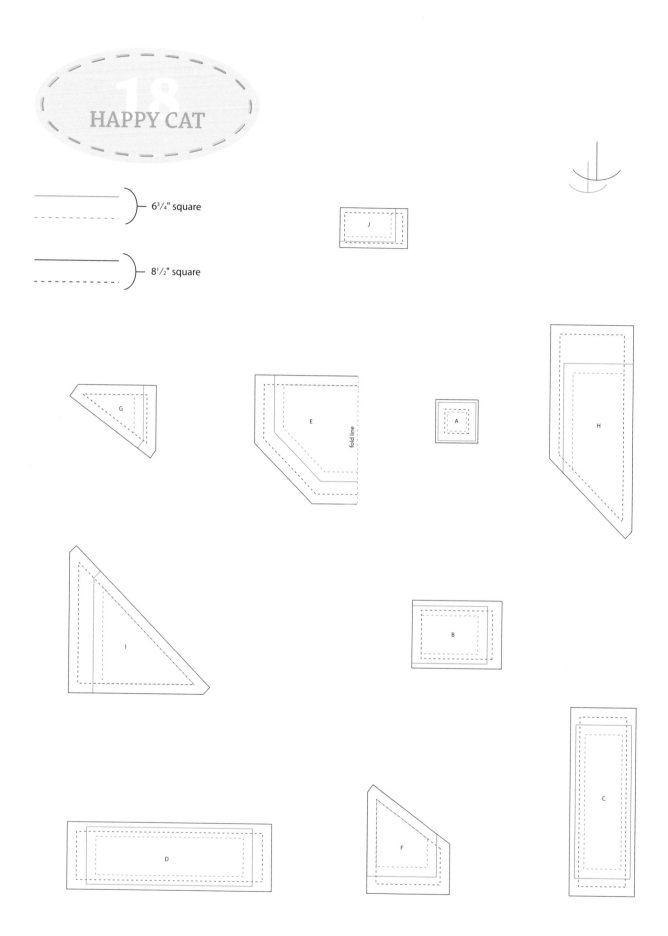

18
HAPPY CAT

6³/₄" square

8¹/₂" square

J

G

E   fold line

A

H

I

B

D

F

C

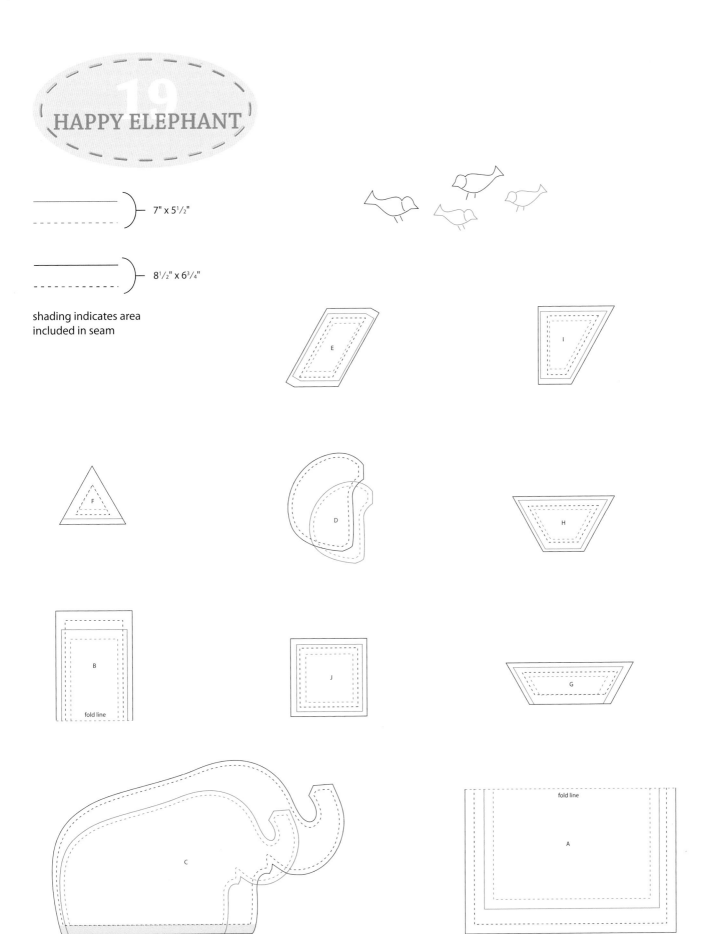

19 HAPPY ELEPHANT

7" x 5½"

8½" x 6¾"

shading indicates area
included in seam

E

I

F

D

H

B

fold line

J

G

C

fold line

A

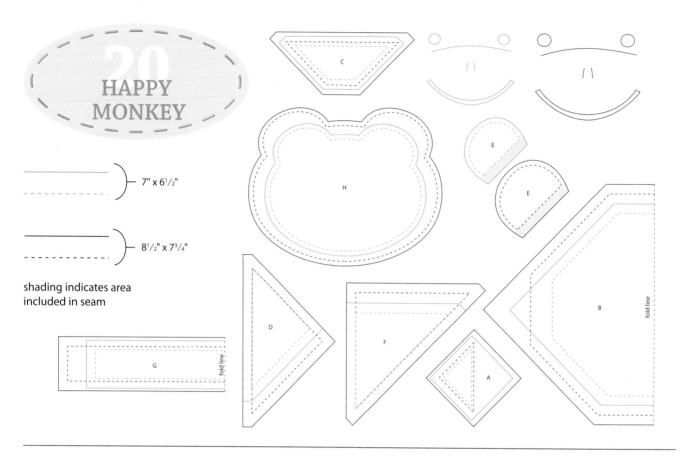

20 HAPPY MONKEY

———— } 7" x 6¹⁄₂"
- - - -

———— } 8¹⁄₂" x 7³⁄₄"
- - - -

shading indicates area
included in seam

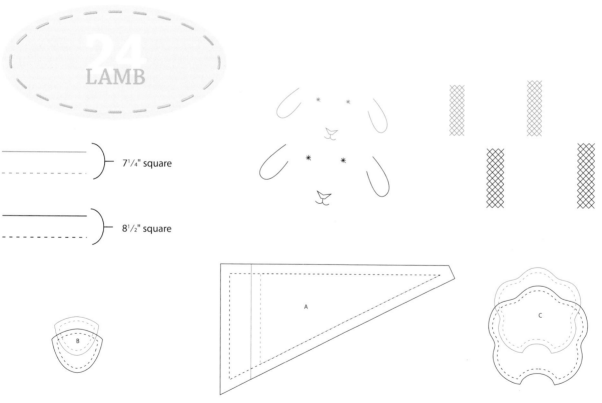

24 LAMB

———— } 7¹⁄₄" square
- - - -

———— } 8¹⁄₂" square
- - - -

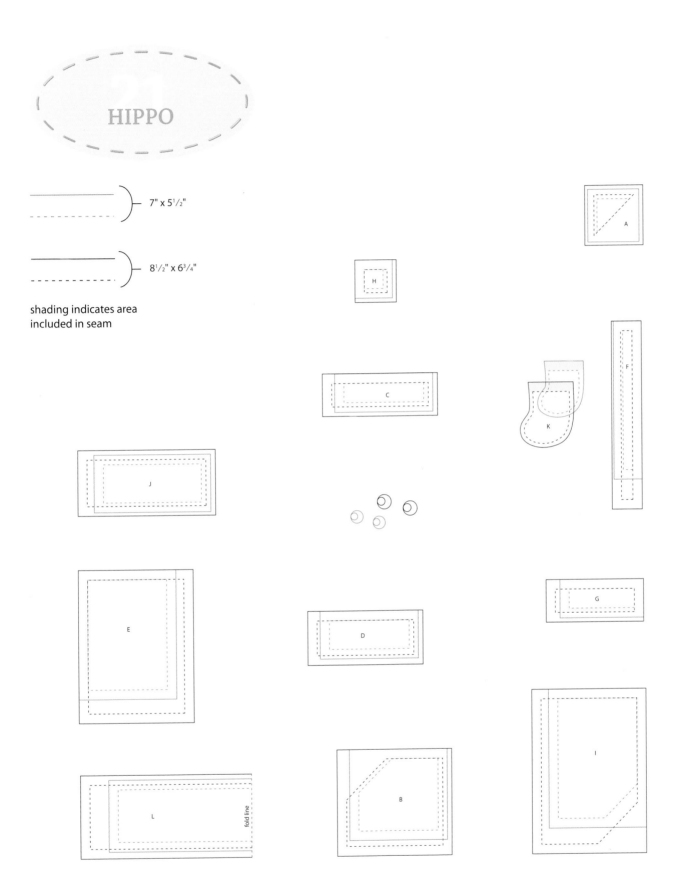

HIPPO

7" x 5$\frac{1}{2}$"

8$\frac{1}{2}$" x 6$\frac{3}{4}$"

shading indicates area
included in seam

A

H

C

F

J

K

E

D

G

L

fold line

B

I

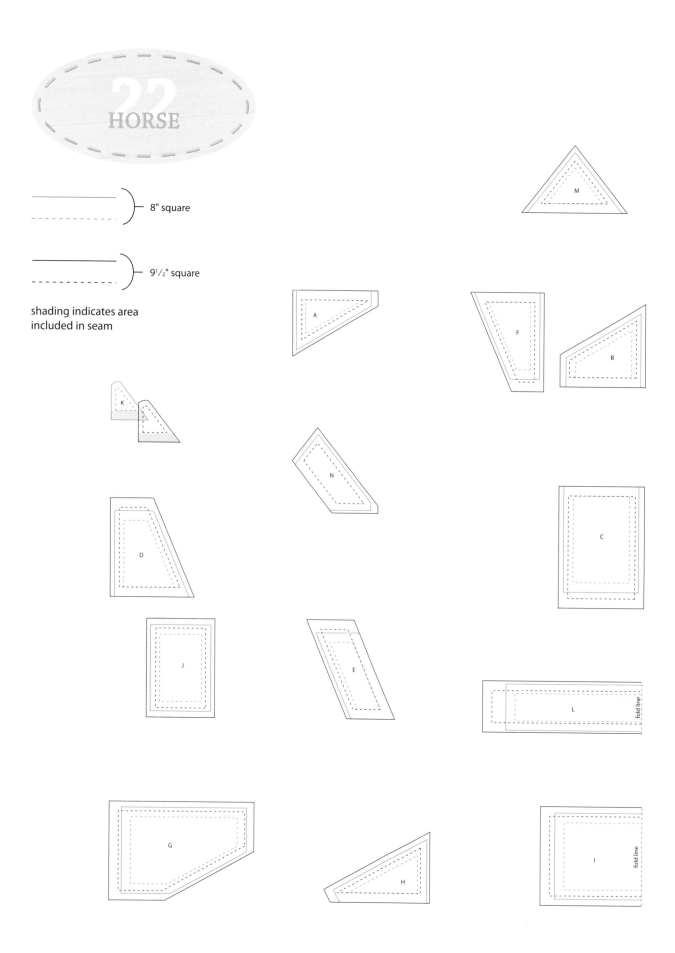

22
HORSE

8" square

9¹/₂" square

shading indicates area
included in seam

A

M

F

B

K

N

C

D

J

E

L
fold line

G

H

I
fold line

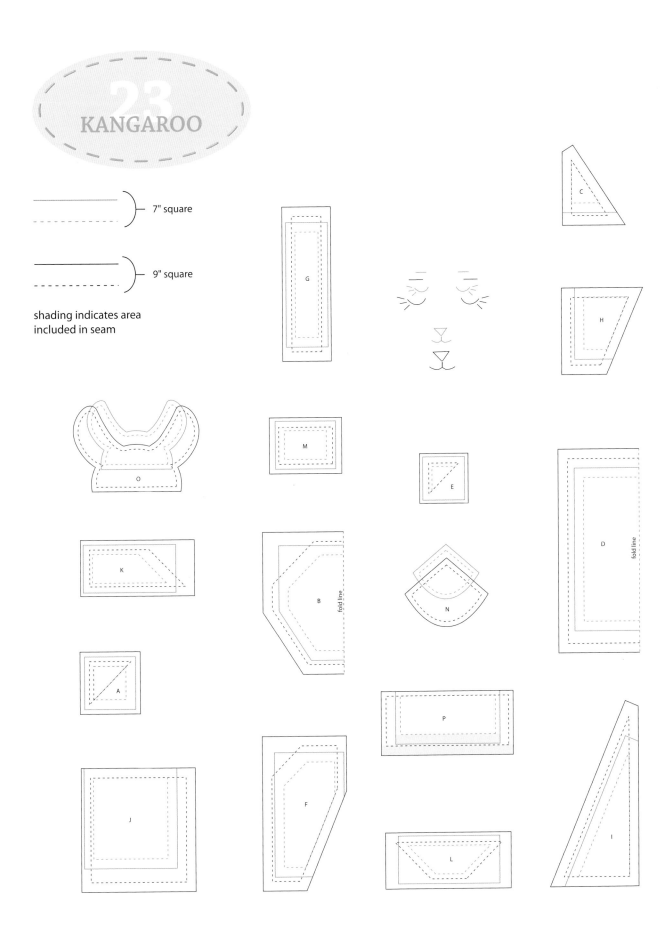

23 KANGAROO

7" square

9" square

shading indicates area
included in seam

G

C

H

M

E

O

K

B

fold line

N

D

fold line

A

J

F

P

L

I

LITTLE BEAR

7¹/₄" x 6¹/₂"

8¹/₂" x 7³/₄"

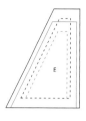

E

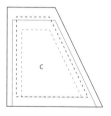

C

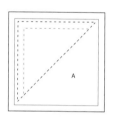

A

B

fold line

F

G

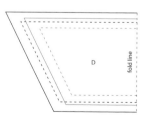

D

fold line

LITTLE CHICK

— 4³/₄" square

— 6" square

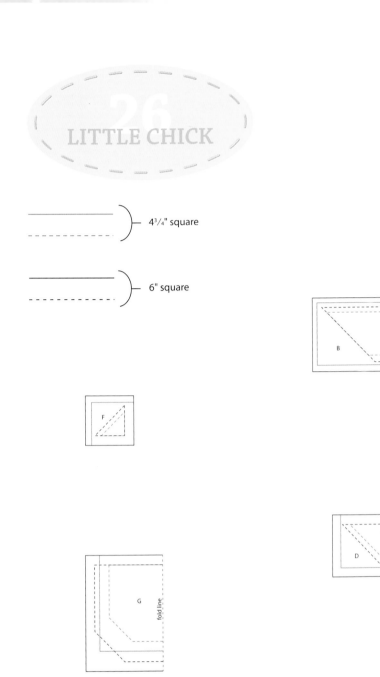

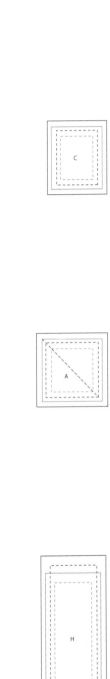

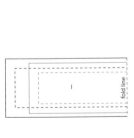

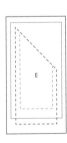

29
PANDA

6¼" square

7½" square

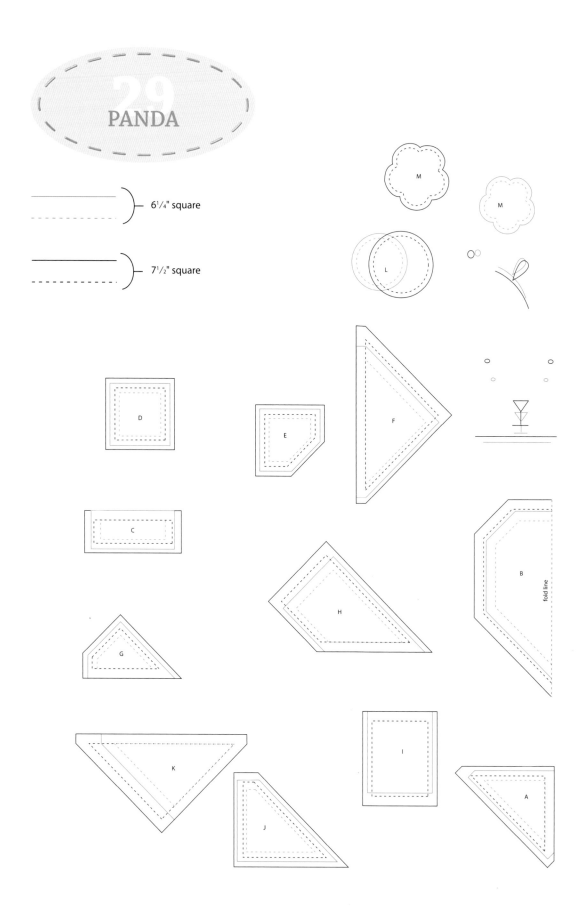

M

M

L

D

E

F

C

H

B

fold line

G

K

I

J

A

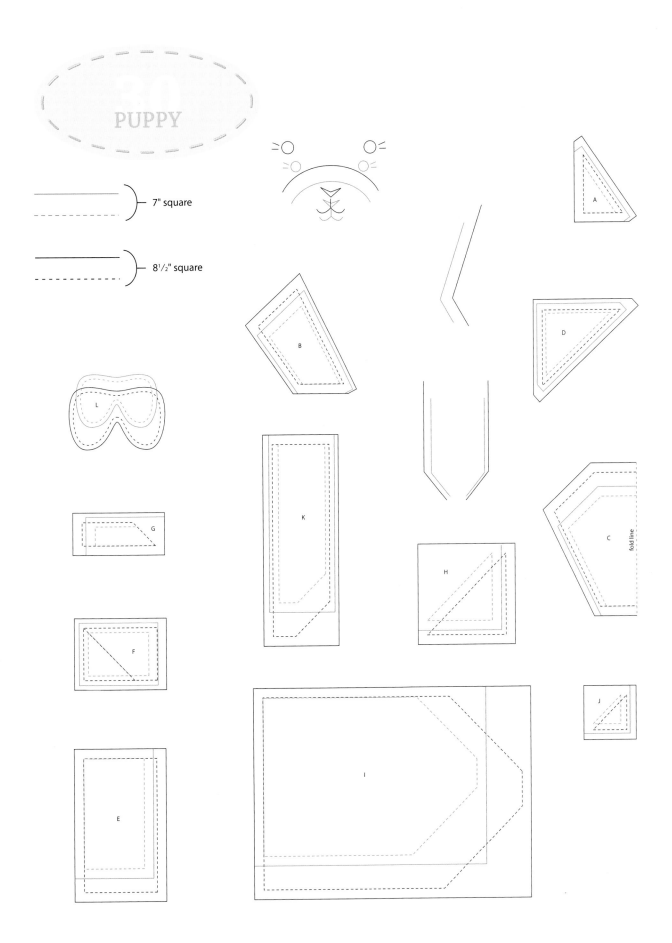

PUPPY

——————— ⊃ 7" square
- - - - - - - - ⊃

——————— ⊃ 8¹/₂" square
- - - - - - - - ⊃

A

B

D

L

C   fold line

G

K

H

J

F

E

I

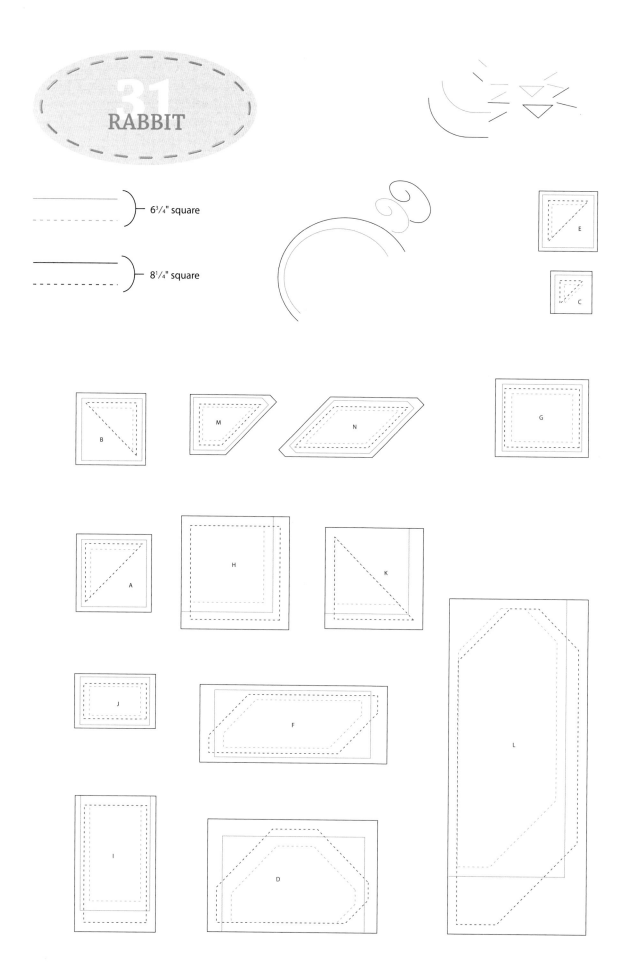

31
RABBIT

6³/₄" square

8¹/₄" square

E

C

B

M

N

G

A

H

K

J

F

L

I

D

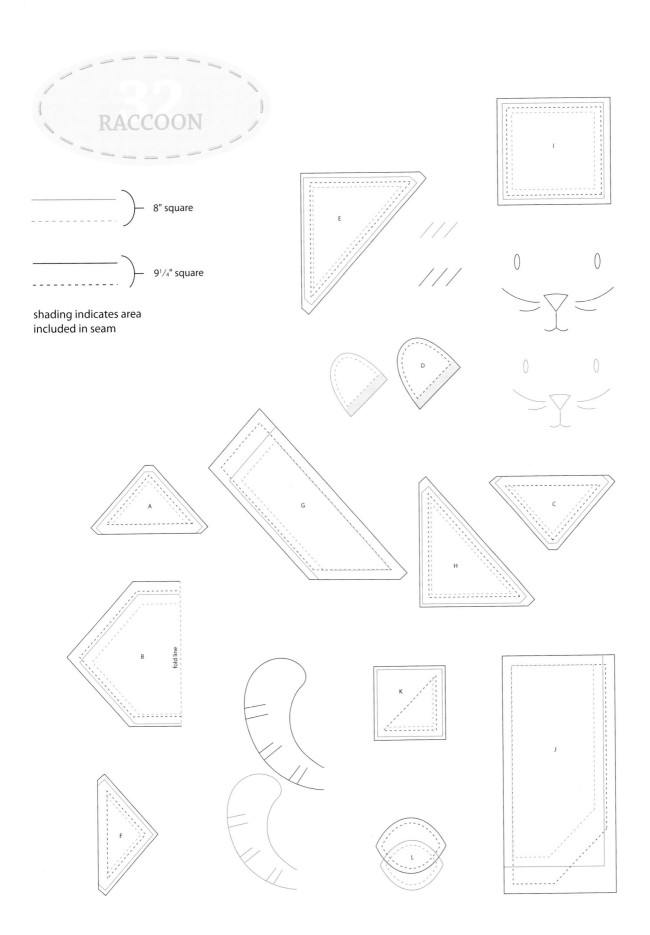

32
RACCOON

8" square

9¼" square

shading indicates area
included in seam

E

I

D

A

G

H

C

B

fold line

K

J

F

L

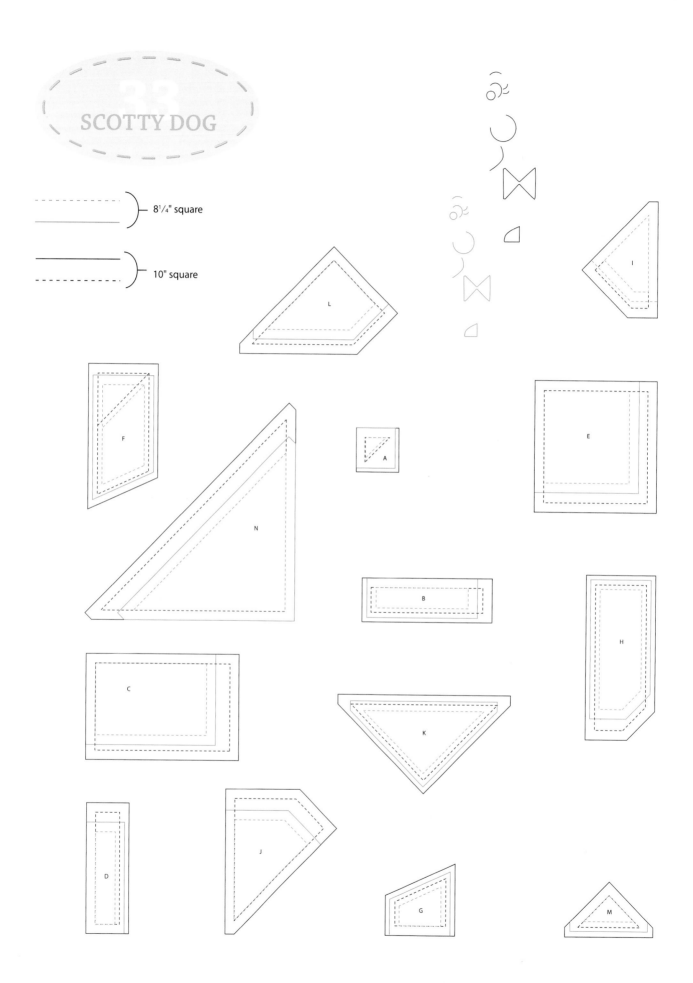

23
SCOTTY DOG

- 8¼" square
- 10" square

SITTING
MONKEY

7" square

8½" square

fold line

J

K

L

I

G

H

A

B

C

F

D

E

SNAKE

6" square

7½" square

shading indicates area
included in seam

A

fold line

B

C

B

F

fold line

E

E

G

G

C

D

D

SITTING CAT

35

—————— 6" x 8½"
- - - - - -

—————— 6¾" x 9½"
- - - - - -

shading indicates area
included in seam

E

A

K

K

J

L

B

D

I

F

H fold line

G

C

37
SQUIRREL

6½" square

8" square

STANDING
CAT

7" square

8½" square

shading indicates area
included in seam

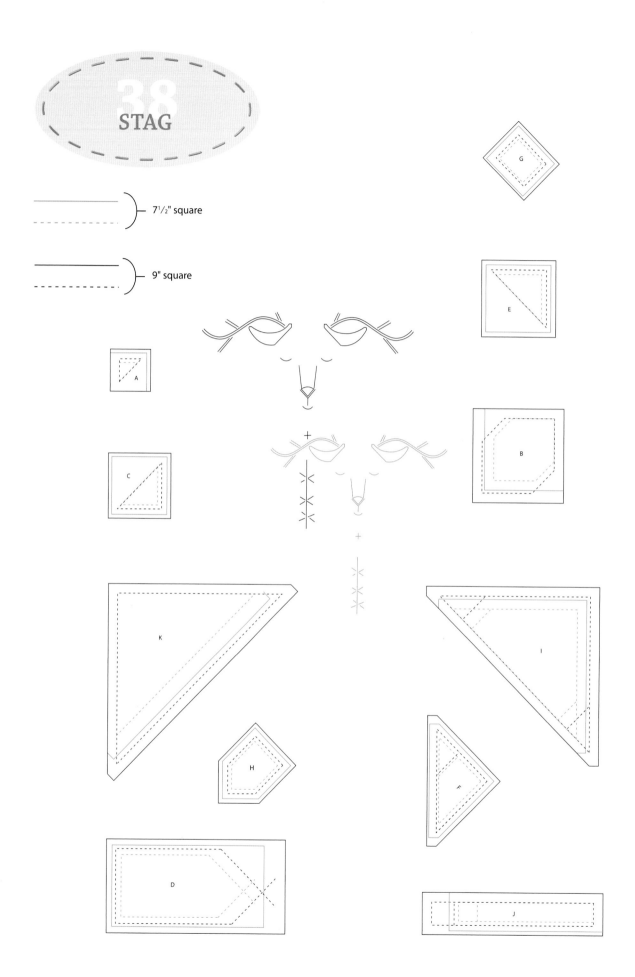

7½" square

9" square

G

E

A

C

B

K

I

H

F

D

J

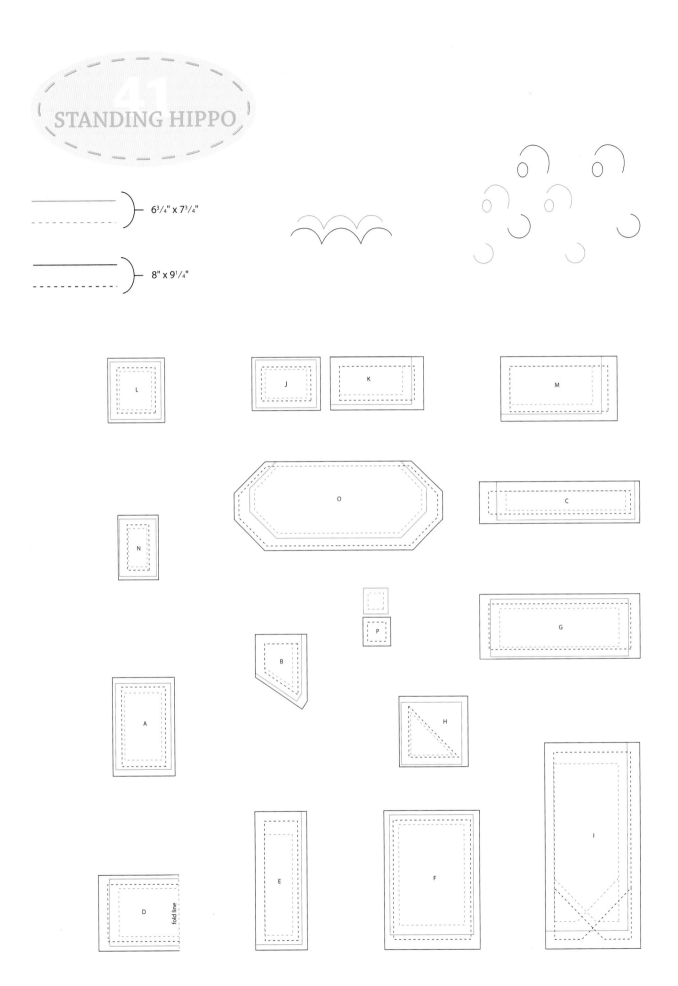

41
STANDING HIPPO

6³/₄" x 7³/₄"

8" x 9¹/₄"

L

J   K   M

N   O   C

P   G

B

A   H

I

E   F

D   fold line

STANDING
LION

— 7" square

— 8¹⁄₂" square

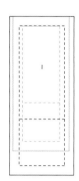

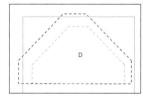

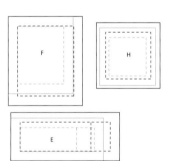

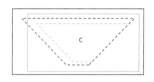

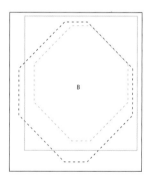

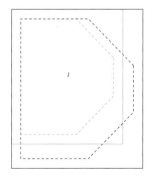

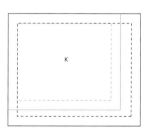

43
TIGER

5¹/₂" x 9"

6¹/₂" x 10¹/₂"

C

R
fold line

F

E

D

B
fold line

L

N

K

A

I

O

P

Q

G

M

J

H

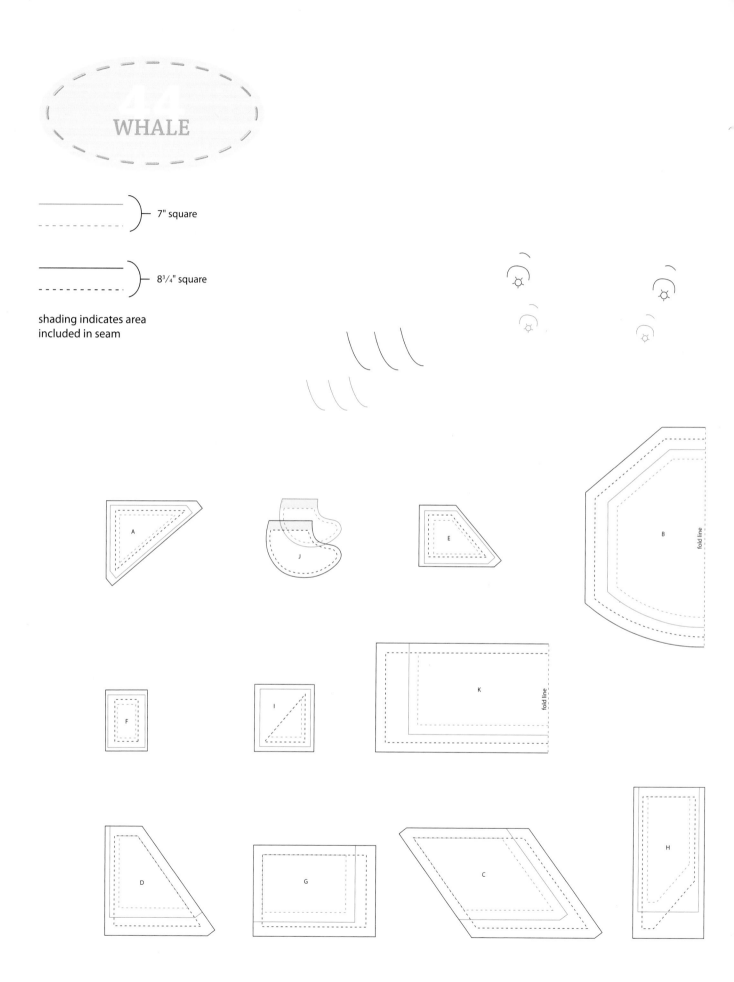

WHALE

7" square

8³/₄" square

shading indicates area
included in seam

A

J

E

B

fold line

F

I

K

fold line

D

G

C

H

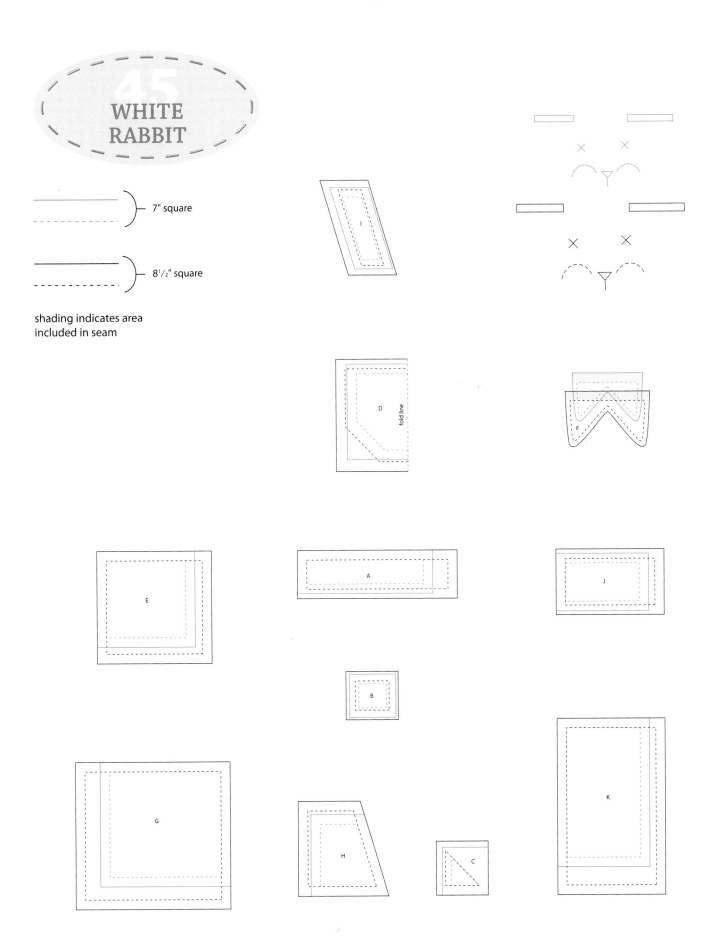

WHITE RABBIT

45

7" square

8¹/₂" square

shading indicates area
included in seam

I

D fold line

F

E

A

J

B

G

H

C

K

Index

Back stitch, 9
Blanket stitch, 9

Chain stitch, 9
Couched stitch, 8
Cross stitch, 8
Curve Patch Piecing, 8

Embroidery, 9

Fabric preparation, 6
Fabric selection, 6
French knot, 9

General instructions, 6

Hand Appliqué, 8

Log cabin border, 8
Long stitch, 9

Machine piecing, 7
Marking tools, 6
Mitered corners, 7

Quilt blocks, 10
1. Baby Elephant, 10
2. Baby Giraffe, 11
3. Bluebird, 12
4. Butterfly, 13
5. Chicken, 14
6. Circus Elephant, 16
7. Cow, 17
8. Crocodile, 18
9. Dancing Monkey, 19
10. Deer, 20
11. Duck, 22
12. Elephant Face, 23
13. Fox, 24
14. Frog, 26
15. Gecko, 27
16. Giraffe, 28
17. Grizzly Bear, 29
18. Happy Cat, 30
19. Happy Elephant, 32
20. Happy Monkey, 33
21. Hippo, 34
22. Horse, 36
23. Kangaroo, 38
24. Lamb, 40

25. Little Bear, 41
26. Little Chick, 42
27. Mouse, 43
28. Owl, 44
29. Panda, 46
30. Puppy, 48
31. Rabbit, 49
32. Raccoon, 50
33. Scotty Dog, 52
34. Sitting Monkey, 53
35. Sitting Cat, 54
36. Snake, 56
37. Squirrel, 57
38. Stag, 58
39. Standing Cat, 60
40. Standing Dog, 61
41. Standing Hippo, 62
42. Standing Lion, 64
43. Tiger, 66
44. Whale, 68
45. White Rabbit, 70

Template preparation, 6
Templates, 72

Running stitch, 9

Satin stitch, 9
Spider web rose, 9
Stem stitch, 9

Wrapped back stitch, 9

Metric Conversion chart

INCHES	MILLIMETERS (MM)/ CENTIMETERS (CM)
1/8	3 mm
3/16	5 mm
1/4	6 mm
5/16	8 mm
3/8	9.5 mm
7/16	1.1 cm
1/2	1.3 cm
7/16	1.4 cm
5/8	1.6 cm
11/16	1.7 cm
3/4	1.9 cm
13/16	2.1 cm
7/8	2.2cm
15/16	2.4 cm
1	2.5 cm
1½	3.8 cm
2	5 cm
2½	6.4 cm
3	7.6 cm
3½	8.9 cm
4	10.2 cm
4½	11.4 cm
5	12.7 cm
5½	14 cm
6	15.2 cm
6½	16.5 cm
7	17.8 cm
7½	19 cm
8	20.3 cm
8½	21.6 cm
9 (¼ yard)	22.9 cm
9½	24.1 cm
10	25.4 cm
10½	26.7 cm
11	27.9 cm
11½	29.2 cm
12	30.5 cm